PENGUIN CLASSICS

THE SONNETS

JORGE LUIS BORGES was born in Buenos Aires in 1899 and was educated in Europe. One of the most widely acclaimed writers of our time, he published many collections of poems, essays, and short stories before his death in Geneva in June 1986. In 1961, Borges shared the International Publisher's Prize with Samuel Beckett. The Ingram Merrill Foundation granted him its Annual Literary Award in 1966 for his "outstanding contribution to literature." In 1971, Columbia University awarded him the first of many degrees of Doctor of Letters, *honoris causa* (eventually the list included both Oxford and Cambridge), that he was to receive from the English-speaking world. In 1971, he also received the fifth biennial Jerusalem Prize and in 1973 was given one of Mexico's most prestigious cultural awards, the Alfonso Reyes Prize. In 1980, he shared with Gerardo Diego the Cervantes Prize, the highest literary accolade of the Spanish-speaking world. Borges was Director of the Argentine National Library from 1955 until 1973.

STEPHEN KESSLER is a poet, translator, essayist, and editor. His previous translations include books by Fernando Alegría, Vicente Aleixandre, Luis Cernuda, Julio Cortázar, Ariel Dorfman, Pablo Neruda, and César Vallejo, among others. He is a major contributor of translations to the other Penguin volumes of the poetry of Jorge Luis Borges, *Selected Poems* and *Poems of the Night*. His recent books include *Burning Daylight* (poems), *Eyeseas* by Raymond Queneau (translation, with Daniela Hurezanu), *Desolation of the Chimera* by Luis Cernuda (translation), and *Moving Targets: On Poets, Poetry & Translation* (essays). He resides in Northern California and is the editor of *The Redwood Coast Review*.

SUZANNE JILL LEVINE, the distinguished translator of such innovative Spanish American writers as Manuel Puig, Guillermo Cabrera Infante, Jorge Luis Borges, and Julio Cortázar, is the author of *The Subversive Scribe: Translating Latin American Fiction* and *Manuel Puig and the Spider Woman: His Life and Fictions*. A professor of Latin American literature and translation studies at the University of California at Santa Barbara, she has been awarded PEN American Center and PEN USA West awards, National Endowment for the Arts and for the Humanities grants, and a Guggenheim Foundation fellowship.

The Translators

Willis Barnstone
Robert Fitzgerald
Edith Grossman
Stephen Kessler
Eric McHenry
W. S. Merwin
Alastair Reid
Hoyt Rogers
Mark Strand
Charles Tomlinson
Alan S. Trueblood
John Updike

JORGE LUIS BORGES

The Sonnets

A DUAL-LANGUAGE EDITION
WITH PARALLEL TEXT

Edited with an Introduction and Notes by
STEPHEN KESSLER

General Editor
SUZANNE JILL LEVINE

PENGUIN BOOKS

PENGUIN BOOKS

Published by the Penguin Group

Penguin Group (USA) Inc., 375 Hudson Street, New York, New York 10014, U.S.A.

Penguin Group (Canada), 90 Eglinton Avenue East, Suite 700, Toronto,
Ontario, Canada M4P 2Y3 (a division of Pearson Penguin Canada Inc.)

Penguin Books Ltd, 80 Strand, London WC2R 0RL, England

Penguin Ireland, 25 St Stephen's Green, Dublin 2, Ireland (a division of Penguin Books Ltd)

Penguin Group (Australia), 250 Camberwell Road, Camberwell,
Victoria 3124, Australia (a division of Pearson Australia Group Pty Ltd)

Penguin Books India Pvt Ltd, 11 Community Centre, Panchsheel Park, New Delhi - 110 017, India

Penguin Group (NZ), 67 Apollo Drive, Rosedale, North Shore 0632,
New Zealand (a division of Pearson New Zealand Ltd)

Penguin Books (South Africa) (Pty) Ltd, 24 Sturdee Avenue,
Rosebank, Johannesburg 2196, South Africa

Penguin Books Ltd, Registered Offices:
80 Strand, London WC2R 0RL, England

First published in Penguin Books 2010

Selection copyright © Maria Kodama, 2010
Translation copyright © Penguin Group (USA) Inc., 2010
Introduction and notes copyright © Stephen Kessler, 2010
All rights reserved

Page 312 constitutes an extension of this copyright page.

LIBRARY OF CONGRESS CATALOGING IN PUBLICATION DATA
Borges, Jorge Luis, 1899–1986.
[Sonnets. English & Spanish]
The sonnets : a dual-language edition with parallel text / Jorge Luis Borges; edited with
an introduction and notes by Stephen Kessler ; general editor, Suzanne Jill Levine.
p. cm.—(Penguin classics)
This collection brings together all of the sonnets of Jorge Luis Borges, including
selections from the author's Obras completas, La cifra, Los conjurados, etc.
Includes bibliographical references and index.
ISBN 978-0-14-310601-2
1. Borges, Jorge Luis, 1899–1986—Translations into English. 2. Sonnets, Argentine—
Translations into English. I. Kessler, Stephen, 1947– II. Levine, Suzanne Jill. III. Title.
PQ7797.B635A2 2010
861'.62—dc22   2010001306

Set in Sabon

146122990

Contents

THE SONNETS

Introduction

The name Jorge Luis Borges evokes, for most readers of English, the image of a master of prose fiction, the experimental writer of highly cerebral proto-postmodernist stories, godfather of "magic realism" and detonator of the "Boom" of Latin American novels of the 1960s—even though Borges himself never wrote a novel. During those years Borges, born in 1899, already revered in Latin America, visited the United States several times, giving lectures and readings at various universities, and came to be known as the slyly self-deprecating and vastly erudite blind Argentine librarian, paradoxically shy even while enjoying in the most sociable manner his newfound international celebrity. One of the things Borges's readers and admirers may or may not have realized at the time was that Borges thought of himself primarily as a poet.

Frail and nearsighted, endlessly absorbed in his father's library, Borges was a bookish child from the beginning. That library was comprised largely of books in English, the first language he learned to read and the native tongue of his paternal grandmother, Frances Haslam. Borges's father, Jorge Guillermo, read aloud to him in English, and Borges locates his literary awakening in the first time his father read to him Keats's "Ode to a Nightingale." He later recalled his sensation as a child of hearing "words that I understood not, but yet I felt." It was their sound that captivated him. "I had thought of language as a way of saying things, of uttering complaints, of saying that one was glad, or sad, and so on. Yet when I heard those lines . . . I knew that language could also be a music and a passion. And thus was poetry revealed to me."

And thus is Borges revealed to us as quite a different writer from the one we thought we knew. This Borges is passionate, lyrical, intoxicated with the sounds of words, and is a prolific poet who produced a 645-page *Obra Poética* in Spanish, some 140 pages of which are sonnets.

In Geneva with his family as an adolescent, young Georgie, as he was called by everyone, discovered German Expressionism, and composed his first poems in English and French—sonnets in imitation of Wordsworth and the Symbolists. In 1919, in Spain, he published his first poems in Spanish under the influence of Rafael Cansinos-Asséns, leader of a movement known as *ultraísmo*. On his return to Buenos Aires in his early twenties, Borges soon outgrew the futuristic-modernist aesthetic of the Expressionists and Ultraists in favor of a more plainspoken, straightforward yet nonetheless musical style, a style he applied to infusing his perceptions of his native city with a metaphysical or mystical aura in his first book, *Fervor de Buenos Aires*, and that he sustained and refined over the next six decades. While he wrote a few sonnets in the 1920s, he didn't include them in his published books, having accepted the notion of the modern enough to adopt free verse as his form of poetic expression. But as he noted later, "We don't have to strive to be modern." By virtue of living, for better or worse, in the twentieth century, "we *are* modern."

The arc of Borges's career as a poet has an odd trajectory. He wrote mostly verse and critical essays through the 1920s, publishing three books of poems by the time he was thirty. Then he set poetry aside, at least for publication, and from the thirties through the fifties, prose—fictions but also all kinds of essays, including those hybrid pieces that blur the distinction between one genre and another—was his main mode of literary creation. As blindness overcame him (it was congenital, inherited from his father, who had also gone blind) he returned to poetry from the late fifties until his death in Geneva in 1986. Blindness, then, brought him full circle—not only back to poetry but also to a more formal style, based on rhyme and meter, than his earlier verse, which had been much influenced by Whitman. (Though Borges's first reading language was English, and later he was to translate Whitman, the first versions he read of the great American bard were in German, done by contemporary Expressionist poets.)

As Borges explained in his "Autobiographical Essay" of 1970: "One salient consequence of my blindness was my gradual abandonment of free verse in favor of classical metrics. In fact, blindness made me take up the writing of poetry again. Since rough drafts were denied to me, I had to fall back on memory. It is obviously easier to remember verse than prose, and to remember regular verse forms rather than free ones. Regular verse is, so to speak, portable. One can walk down the street or be riding the subway while composing and polishing a sonnet, for rhyme and meter have mnemonic virtues."

And so, this book is a portable Borges, for not only is the sonnet a portable form but in his sonnets Borges distills all the obsessive themes that pervade his other writings—the mirror, the labyrinth, the garden, the dream, the soldier, the hoodlum, history, oblivion, memory, ancestors, time, eternity, literary and philosophical forebears—into the gemlike form of fourteen tightly rhymed lines. In his sonnets, almost all of them written in the last twenty-five years of his life (and arranged here chronologically, as presented in his books), the poet turns both Petrarchan and Shakespearean traditions to his own purposes, as lyrics of praise ("Wine Sonnet," "Of the Lovely and Varied Andalusia"), reflective meditations ("Rain," "I Am"), songs of longing ("New England, 1967," "The Day Before"), dramatic mini-monologues ("The Inquisitor," "The Conqueror"), contemplations of place ("Texas," "Buenos Aires"), acts of personal and historical commemoration ("Allusion to a Shade of the Eighteen-nineties," "To a Saxon Poet"), addresses to and invocations of other writers ("Edgar Allan Poe," "A Rose and Milton"), evocations of domestic mysteries ("The Mirror," "Things"), excursions into mythology ("Proteus," "A Bust of Janus Speaks") and theology ("The Other," "He"), philosophical inquiries ("Everness," "We Are Rivers"), or metaphysical speculations ("Cosmogony," "Clouds").

The Petrarchan or Italian model of the sonnet is typically made up of two quatrains, or an octave, and two tercets, or a sestet, a structure that shifts after the introductory eight lines to a conclusion in the final six, with distinct rhyme patterns in each part of the poem (traditionally abba-abba and cde-cde). The Shakespearean or English model is commonly made up of three quatrains (abab-cdcd-efef) and a couplet (gg), with the closing rhymed lines summarizing the poem's argument. Borges adheres strictly to neither of these models but uses them as structural frameworks for his own variations (usually rhymed abba-cddc-eef-ggf or abba-cddc-effe-gg).

True to his range of thematic and rhetorical purposes, Borges follows no consistent pattern of rhyme, line length (while he most commonly uses the classical Spanish eleven-syllable line, he sometimes extends the line to a thirteen- to fifteen-syllable hexameter), or the traditional structure of his sonnets' arguments. Sometimes he "turns" the poem at the ninth line as in the Italian model, sometimes he summarizes in the final couplet as in Shakespeare, but at other times he lets the poem take its own organic form within the sonic framework of its rhymes ("What Is Lost," "The Day Before"). He has no rhetorical ax to grind, no formally "Borgesian sonnet" to propagate, but uses the abundance of rhyme in Spanish to knit its sounds together and move his compositional process along by melodic association. He is building a brief song. Less concerned with following a formula than with condensing his thoughts and feelings into concise units of memorable language, Borges in the sonnet brings the verbal economy of his short stories to its most acute realization ("Labyrinth," "The Sum").

Borges the poet is at times far more intimate and personal a writer than Borges the prose narrator. As "autobiographical" as the latter may be in terms of working out his personal obsessions through historical or imaginary characters, the former at his most intimate speaks in a first-person voice inseparable from that of the author. He shares his puzzlement at his identity ("All Our Yesterdays"), his despair at the futility of writing ("Buenos Aires, 1899"), his admiration for other writers and thinkers and his certainty of their enduring value ("To John Keats"), his wonder at the mystery of existence ("The Simple Man"), his nostalgic associations with the Buenos Aires of his youth ("J. M."), his paradoxical longings for both oblivion and immortality ("The Enigmas"), in musings that, while no less intellectual than his other writings, seem to arise from the deepest part of the self and speak from the heart's most urgent necessity.

Yet true to his contradictions, Borges is also the most objective of poets, and the most sympathetic, sketching the lives and exploring the consciousness of historical figures ("Jonathan Edwards"), soldiers ("One of Lee's Soldiers"), hoodlums ("Dead Hoodlums"), ancestors ("The Borges"), and animals ("The Panther"); engaging in dialogues with and meditations on dead friends ("Ricardo

Güiraldes"), philosophers ("Emanuel Swedenborg"), and fictional characters in works of art ("Blind Pew"). To be sure, there are pro forma exercises that have about them an air of duty or routine, the poet turning out his daily allotment of lines. But in a surprisingly large percentage of these poems, even the most "impersonal" ones, we hear a Borges who is earnest, reflective, vulnerable, less ironic than the subtle trickster of the fictions, a man with the same uncertainties and insecurities as anyone else but with the technical confidence to refine them precisely and with a feeling of solace in the act of creation.

"The central fact of my life," he said in his lecture "A Poet's Creed," delivered at Harvard in 1968, "has been the existence of words and the possibility of weaving those words into poetry. At first, certainly, I was only a reader. Yet I think the happiness of a reader is beyond that of a writer, for a reader need feel no trouble, no anxiety: he is merely out for happiness." In another lecture on poetry, published in the collection *Seven Nights*, he describes his approach to the teaching of literature: "Why not study the texts directly? If you like the book, fine; if you don't, don't read it. The idea of compulsory reading is absurd; it's only worthwhile to speak of compulsory happiness. I believe that poetry is something one feels. If you don't feel poetry, if you have no sense of beauty, if a story doesn't make you want to know what happens next, then the author has not written for you."

This gives us a clue to our own reading of these poems, and how Borges would like us to experience them: for pleasure. He speaks often throughout his writings of the joyful enchantment of immersion in the imagination of another artist or writer, especially the sensory and sentimental gratifications of poetry. Sentiment—felt thought, not sentimentality—denotes Borges's romantic impulses restrained, his simultaneous indulgence in and resistance to the pull of nostalgia, his worship of and skepticism toward the beautiful. Even the romance of physical courage and the fascination with violence, which he indulges in his salutes to military figures and turn-of-the-century Buenos Aires knife-fighters, are ultimately, for a physically timid bookworm like himself, nothing compared to the allure of song and the excitement of language made magical by the poet's art. That sense of magic is nowhere more concentrated than in the sonnets.

Collected here for the first time in one volume—more than half of them newly translated into English*—Borges's sonnets open fresh perspectives into the life and work of one of the world's best-known and most studied authors. The previously published translations in this book are all taken from Alexander Coleman's 1999 Penguin edition of Borges's *Selected Poems*. Most of the new translations are based on the sonnets in the 2005 *Obra Poética* published in Argentina by Emecé. As Borges was known to revise his poems with each edition, and some of the translators were working at different times from different texts, I've made no attempt to reconcile the variations in capitalization, punctuation, stanza breaks or other incidental inconsistencies, as the substance of the poems is fairly constant from one edition to the next.

The poems in the section headed "Uncollected Sonnets" are taken from three volumes of posthumously published *Textos Recobrados* and generally come from very early or very late in the poet's life. One can never be sure with Borges when a previously undiscovered text will turn up, but this is as close to a "complete" collection of his sonnets as we are likely to have. (For dates of uncollected sonnets and a note on completeness, see the Notes starting on page 302.)

While the bulk of the translations in this book were done by Alastair Reid, Willis Barnstone, and myself, nine other poets and translators have also contributed, each with an individual approach to the formal challenge of the sonnet and how to render it in language that is both a reliable representation of the original and a persuasive poem in English for the contemporary reader. Borges, who was himself a translator (of Whitman, Kafka, Faulkner, Joyce, Virginia Woolf, and others), often spoke of literary translation as re-creation, and of the translator's responsibility to improve on the original if necessary, including the duty to be "unfaithful" in the interest of bringing out qualities latent in the text (an example would be Alastair Reid's version of "Religio Medici, 1643," but the attentive bilingual reader will surely find others). This is perilous territory, for it assumes the translator is the artistic equal of the

---

* Seventy-nine of these one hundred thirty-seven poems are new translations: two by Alastair Reid, four by Edith Grossman, and the rest by the editor.

author, yet that is the leap any translator must take in recreating a work of imagination.

The sonnet's strictly formal characteristics—fourteen lines with a fixed pattern of end rhyme and a measure in English of roughly five beats or ten syllables per line (iambic pentameter)—impose their own demands, and different translators hear these patterns and their meanings differently, leading them to invent different responses. These range from a meticulous formalism that attempts to replicate the metric and rhyme scheme of the original—a daunting challenge given the much greater richness of rhyme in Spanish and the risk of sacrificing meaning to form—to a more relaxed approximation of the technical aspects of the sonnet in search of a poem that sounds less self-consciously artificial in English. In practice, even the most rigorous exponents of formal verse vary the tempo and syllabic stresses of regular measures like iambic pentameter to avoid a metronomic monotony (see Shakespeare, Milton, Shelley, Hopkins, and countless others); in the most accomplished formal writers, like Yeats or Dylan Thomas, their technical skill is hidden in the seemingly natural movement of the lines. Interestingly, the most renowned poets represented as translators in this volume, W. S. Merwin, Charles Tomlinson, and Mark Strand, seem the least concerned with the purely formal properties of the sonnet. Other comparably distinguished writers like Robert Fitzgerald, John Updike, and Willis Barnstone anchor their versions in a more strictly structural fidelity.

In any case, there is no such thing as a definitive translation—Borges was known to say that even an original work of literature is never definitive. The ideal translator is akin to Pierre Menard, the protagonist of Borges's famous story who rewrites, word for word, a *Don Quixote* identical to but somehow different from the original—a version that might even be a slight improvement. Another Borgesian ideal for a book like this one would be a tome of infinite pages with an infinite number of translators each doing a version of every poem. The reader of such a book would discover not only the astonishing variability in even the most faithful translations but also the multitude of readings of each poem. Each reader would be inspired to arrive at his own reading, perhaps a composite of all the others, or even a new translation of his own.

But such a book exists only in a parallel literary universe—like Borges's Library of Babel—and we must settle for a more finite and approximate embodiment of the sonnets. An example of even the author "translating" one of his own poems is "You Are Not the Others" (page 241) and "The Speck" (page 259), identical texts except for their titles, published by Borges in two different books, which here have been rendered by Eric McHenry and myself, respectively. McHenry takes the more formal approach, skillfully approximating the original rhyme scheme, while my version places greater emphasis on rhythm and internal or off-rhymes to create an illusion of what might be called *sonnetude*. Both translations may be equally true to the letter and spirit of the originals, but the difference between them serves to illustrate how distinct from each other two versions of the same text can be.

The most avid readers will want to seek out other versions of as many of the sonnets as possible, both as a way of reading them more deeply and of discovering aspects of the poems that may be absent from any one translation. I would also encourage readers with even rudimentary Spanish to read the original language and see for themselves some of the interpretive riddles translators routinely must try to untangle. More than a matter of getting the words or themes or literal meanings right, the best translations catch the style and tone and mood and atmosphere of a poem to give the reader something like the *experience* of the original. Other books in which Borges's sonnets (including some of these) can be found in English include *Six Masters of the Spanish Sonnet* by Willis Barnstone; *Selected Poems, 1923–1967* of Jorge Luis Borges, edited by Norman Thomas di Giovanni; *Borges: A Reader*, edited by Emir Rodríguez Monegal and Alastair Reid; and *Jorge Luis Borges: A Personal Anthology*, edited by Anthony Kerrigan. The fertility of the originals will be ever more apparent.

As if to prove the protean multiplicity of his own creative identity, Borges appears in his sonnets to be a different author from the radical innovator of his fictions. The storyteller famed for liberating modern literature in Spanish from the limits of the European tradition is revealed here as the reverent guardian of the very traditions he spent much of his career subverting and transforming. The Borges of the sonnets is a deeply conservative poet whose voice, even in Spanish, often sounds more British than Latin American. This is surely due to his lifelong immersion in English literature, and the stately old-world register of his poetic voice. Unlike his contemporaries Pablo Neruda and César Vallejo, widely regarded as the most important South American poets of their time, Borges in his poetry—as distinct from the deep originality of his fiction—has little interest in "making it new," and little use for that doctrine's leading proponent, Ezra Pound. Borges the fabulist may have turned modern fiction inside out, but Borges the poet, especially in the sonnets, "made it old" in a way that continues to feel timeless. This Borgesian paradox only enriches our understanding of one of the twentieth century's greatest writers.

STEPHEN KESSLER

Acknowledgments

Numerous individuals—scholars, poets, editors, translators, and friends—have made vital contributions, in one form or another, to the completion of this volume.

Suzanne Jill Levine has been of immense help in her early and ongoing critical support, encouragement, and editorial work with me on new translations. Efraín Kristal's knowledge of Borges and his influences, his understanding of the sonnets, his book on Borges and translation, *Invisible Work*, and his reading of and thoughts on individual poems have been immeasurably helpful. Carolyn Tipton's correspondence and conversations with me on the history of the sonnet have contributed much to my understanding of the tradition. Alastair Reid's translations and his insights into Borges as a poet have been a model and an inspiration.

Willis Barnstone's work (in *Six Masters of the Spanish Sonnet* and his other writings on Borges) has provided valuable background and anecdotal information on Borges in relation to the sonnet. Paul Oppenheimer (in his book *The Birth of the Modern Mind*) has likewise provided much useful historical information on the origin and evolution of the sonnet. Norman Thomas di Giovanni and Alexander Coleman, in their respective editions of *Selected Poems* of Borges, laid the groundwork for and provided many of the translations in this book.

Biographies of Borges by Emir Rodríguez Monegal and Edwin Williamson have proved immensely useful to my understanding of the life of the poet and the historical context of his work.

I am grateful also to bookseller Jesse Case of Santa Cruz, who searched and found for me a number of volumes by and about Borges, and on the sonnet, which proved essential to the realization of this project. Typing assistance from Dorothy Ruef has saved me a good deal of effort. And the encouragement, support, and patience of my wife, translator and scholar Daniela Hurezanu, have been invaluable.

STEPHEN KESSLER

The Sonnets

EL HACEDOR

THE MAKER

(1960)

AJEDREZ

I

En su grave rincón, los jugadores
rigen las lentas piezas. El tablero
los demora hasta el alba en su severo
ámbito en que se odian dos colores.

Adentro irradian mágicos rigores
las formas: torre homérica, ligero
caballo, armada reina, rey postrero,
oblicuo alfil y peones agresores.

Cuando los jugadores se hayan ido,
cuando el tiempo los haya consumido,
ciertamente no habrá cesado el rito.

En el Oriente se encendió esta guerra
cuyo anfiteatro es hoy toda la tierra.
Como el otro, este juego es infinito.

CHESS

I

Set in their studious corners, the players
move the gradual pieces. Until dawn
the chessboard keeps them in its strict confinement
with its two colors set at daggers drawn.

Within the game itself the forms give off
their magic rules: Homeric castle, knight
swift to attack, queen warlike, king decisive,
slanted bishop, and attacking pawns.

Eventually, when the players have withdrawn,
when time itself has finally consumed them,
the ritual certainly will not be done.

It was in the East this war took fire.
Today the whole earth is its theater.
Like the game of love, this game goes on forever.

II

Tenue rey, sesgo alfil, encarnizada
reina, torre directa y peón ladino
sobre lo negro y blanco del camino
buscan y libran su batalla armada.

No saben que la mano señalada
del jugador gobierna su destino,
no saben que un rigor adamantino
sujeta su albedrío y su jornada.

También el jugador es prisionero
(la sentencia es de Omar) de otro tablero
de negras noches y de blancos días.

Dios mueve al jugador, y éste, la pieza.
¿Qué dios detrás de Dios la trama empieza
de polvo y tiempo y sueño y agonías?

II

Faint-hearted king, sly bishop, ruthless queen,
straightforward castle, and deceitful pawn—
over the checkered black and white terrain
they seek out and begin their armed campaign.

They do not know it is the player's hand
that dominates and guides their destiny.
They do not know an adamantine fate
controls their will and lays the battle plan.

The player too is captive of caprice
(the words are Omar's) on another ground
where black nights alternate with whiter days.

God moves the player, he in turn the piece.
But what god beyond God begins the round
of dust and time and sleep and agonies?

—A.R.

SUSANA SOCA

Con lento amor miraba los dispersos
colores de la tarde. Le placía
perderse en la compleja melodía
o en la curiosa vida de los versos.
No el rojo elemental sino los grises
hilaron su destino delicado,
hecho a discriminar y ejercitado
en la vacilación y en los matices.
Sin atreverse a hollar este perplejo
laberinto, atisbaba desde afuera
las formas, el tumulto y la carrera,
como aquella otra dama del espejo.
Dioses que moran más allá del ruego
la abandonaron a ese tigre, el Fuego.

SUSANA SOCA

With lingering love she watched the sunset
spreading its colors. She would lose herself
with pleasure in a complex melody
or in the mystery of a poem's art.
Her destiny was delicately spun
not from primary red but shades of gray,
wrought with careful taste and acted on
with hesitation and with subtlety.
Not daring to set foot in this perplexing
labyrinth, she looked in from outside
at the turmoil, the forms and the ambition,
much like that other lady in the mirror.
Gods that dwell beyond the reach of prayer
abandoned her to that wild tiger, Fire.

—S.K.

LA LLUVIA

Bruscamente la tarde se ha aclarado
porque ya cae la lluvia minuciosa.
Cae o cayó. La lluvia es una cosa
que sin duda sucede en el pasado.

Quien la oye caer ha recobrado
el tiempo en que la suerte venturosa
le reveló una flor llamada *rosa*
y el curioso color del colorado.

Esta lluvia que ciega los cristales
alegrará en perdidos arrabales
las negras uvas de una parra en cierto

patio que ya no existe. La mojada
tarde me trae la voz, la voz deseada,
de mi padre que vuelve y que no ha muerto.

RAIN

Quite suddenly the evening clears at last
as now outside the soft small rain is falling.
Falling or fallen. Rain itself is something
undoubtedly which happens in the past.

Whoever hears it falling has remembered
a time in which a curious twist of fate
brought back to him a flower whose name was "rose"
and the perplexing redness of its red.

This rain which spreads its blind across the pane
must also brighten in forgotten suburbs
the black grapes on a vine across a shrouded

patio now no more. The evening's rain
brings me the voice, the dear voice of my father,
who comes back now, who never has been dead.

—A.R.

A LA EFIGIE DE UN CAPITÁN
DE LOS EJÉRCITOS DE CROMWELL

No rendirán de Marte las murallas
a éste, que salmos del Señor inspiran;
desde otra luz (desde otro siglo) miran
los ojos, que miraron las batallas.
La mano está en los hierros de la espada.
Por la verde región anda la guerra;
detrás de la penumbra está Inglaterra,
y el caballo y la gloria y tu jornada.
Capitán, los afanes son engaños,
vano el arnés y vana la porfía
del hombre, cuyo término es un día;
todo ha concluido hace ya muchos años.
El hierro que ha de herirte se ha herrumbrado;
estás (como nosotros) condenado.

TO THE IMAGE OF A CAPTAIN
IN CROMWELL'S ARMIES

Stone walls of the god of war will not defeat
this man inspired by psalms of the Lord;
from another light (another age) your eyes
look out at us, eyes that took in battles.
Your hand rests on the iron of your sword.
The whole green region is swarming with war;
and beyond all this darkness there is England,
and your horse and the glory of your time.
Captain, zeal and passion are illusion,
armor is vanity, as is the tireless drive
of man, whose term is no more than a day;
everything now is long since gone and done.
The iron made to wound you rusts away;
you are (like all the rest of us) condemned.

—S.K.

A UN VIEJO POETA

Caminas por el campo de Castilla
y casi no lo ves. Un intrincado
versículo de Juan es tu cuidado
y apenas reparaste en la amarilla

puesta del sol. La vaga luz delira
y en el confín del Este se dilata
esa luna de escarnio y de escarlata
que es acaso el espejo de la Ira.

Alzas los ojos y la miras. Una
memoria de algo que fue tuyo empieza
y se apaga. La pálida cabeza

bajas y sigues caminando triste,
sin recordar el verso que escribiste:
Y su epitafio la sangrienta luna.

TO AN OLD POET

You wander through the landscape of Castile
and nearly do not see it. An intricate
verse of John is all you care about
and the yellow sunset is scarcely real

to you. The hazy light is delirious
and at the edge of the East rises a moon
dripping with mockery and scarlet hued
which could perhaps be Anger's mirror image.

You raise your eyes to take it in. A memory
of something that was yours begins to burn
and is extinguished. You bow your pale head

and go on sadly walking down the road
not quite remembering the line you wrote:
And his epitaph the blood-soaked moon.

—S.K.

BLIND PEW

Lejos del mar y de la hermosa guerra,
que así el amor lo que ha perdido alaba,
el bucanero ciego fatigaba
los terrosos caminos de Inglaterra.

Ladrado por los perros de las granjas,
pifia de los muchachos del poblado,
dormía un achacoso y agrietado
sueño en el negro polvo de las zanjas.

Sabía que en remotas playas de oro
era suyo un recóndito tesoro
y esto aliviaba su contraria suerte;

a ti también, en otras playas de oro,
te aguarda incorruptible tu tesoro:
la vasta y vaga y necesaria muerte.

BLIND PEW

Far from the sea and from the beautiful war,
the way love praises what is long since lost,
the sightless buccaneer was wearing down
the dirt and grime of England's cloddy roads.

Barked at by the dogs guarding the farms,
jeered by the boys in all the villages,
what sleep he caught was sickly, troubled, cracked
sleep in the black dust of the roadside ditches.

He knew that on some far-off golden beaches
a hidden treasure waited just for him,
and this was some relief for his hard fate;

and for you, on other golden beaches,
your incorruptible treasure also waits:
vast, mysterious, inevitable death.

— S.K.

ALUSIÓN A UNA SOMBRA DE MIL OCHOCIENTOS NOVENTA Y TANTOS

Nada. Sólo el cuchillo de Muraña.
Sólo en la tarde gris la historia trunca.
No sé por qué en las tardes me acompaña
ese asesino que no he visto nunca.
Palermo era más bajo. El amarillo
paredón de la cárcel dominaba
arrabal y barrial. Por esa brava
región anduvo el sórdido cuchillo.
El cuchillo. La cara se ha borrado
y de aquel mercenario cuyo austero
oficio era el coraje, no ha quedado
más que una sombra y un fulgor de acero.
Que el tiempo, que los mármoles empaña,
salve este firme nombre, Juan Muraña.

ALLUSION TO A SHADE OF THE EIGHTEEN-NINETIES

Nothing remains. Only Muraña's knife.
In the gray twilight only the cut-off story.
Why that assassin I have never seen
comes to me these evenings, I don't know.
Palermo was lower then. The yellow
stone wall of the prison towered over
the slums and muddy streets. Across that tough
neighborhood roamed the cruel, sordid knife.
The knife. The human face has been erased
from the shape of the hired killer whose austere
calling was courage, nothing else is left
but a dark shadow and a flash of steel.
May time and marble's hardness hold his fame.
Remember: Juan Muraña was his name.

—S.K.

ALUSIÓN A LA MUERTE
DEL CORONEL FRANCISCO BORGES
(1833–1874)

Lo dejo en el caballo, en esa hora
crepuscular en que buscó la muerte;
que de todas las horas de su suerte
ésta perdure, amarga y vencedora.
Avanza por el campo la blancura
del caballo y del poncho. La paciente
muerte acecha en los rifles. Tristemente
Francisco Borges va por la llanura.
Esto que lo cercaba, la metralla,
esto que ve, la pampa desmedida,
es lo que vio y oyó toda la vida.
Está en lo cotidiano, en la batalla.
Alto lo dejo en su épico universo
y casi no tocado por el verso.

ALLUSION TO THE DEATH
OF COLONEL FRANCISCO BORGES
(1833–1874)

I leave him on his horse, in that twilight
hour when he went looking for his death;
of all the hours of his fate, may this
one last, victorious and bitter.
In his white poncho on his white horse
he rides across the countryside. Death waits
patiently set to spring from the rifles. Sadly
Francisco Borges crosses the vast plain.
What's aimed to take him down, the fusillade,
what he can see, the pampa's flat expanse,
are what he has heard and seen his whole life long.
He is in battle, at his daily task.
I leave him high in his epic universe
all but untouchable by lines of verse.

—S.K.

LOS BORGES

Nada o muy poco sé de mis mayores
portugueses, los Borges: vaga gente
que prosigue en mi carne, oscuramente,
sus hábitos, rigores y temores.
Tenues como si nunca hubieran sido
y ajenos a los trámites del arte,
indescifrablemente forman parte
del tiempo, de la tierra y del olvido.
Mejor así. Cumplida la faena,
son Portugal, son la famosa gente
que forzó las murallas del Oriente
y se dio al mar y al otro mar de arena.
Son el rey que en el místico desierto
se perdió y el que jura que no ha muerto.

THE BORGES

I know little or nothing of the Borges,
my Portuguese forebears. They were a ghostly line,
who still ply in my body their mysterious
disciplines, habits, and anxieties.
Shadowy, as if they had never been,
and strangers to the processes of art,
indecipherably they form a part
of time, of earth, and of oblivion.
Better so. When everything is said,
they are Portugal, they are that famous people
who forced the Great Wall of the East, and fell
to the sea, and to that other sea of sand.
They are that king lost on the mystic strand
and those at home who swear he is not dead.

—A.R.

A LUIS DE CAMOËNS

Sin lástima y sin ira el tiempo mella
las heroicas espadas. Pobre y triste
a tu patria nostálgica volviste,
oh capitán, para morir en ella
y con ella. En el mágico desierto
la flor de Portugal se había perdido
y el áspero español, antes vencido,
amenazaba su costado abierto.
Quiero saber si aquende la ribera
última comprendiste humildemente
que todo lo perdido, el Occidente
y el Oriente, el acero y la bandera,
perduraría (ajeno a toda humana
mutación) en tu Eneida lusitana.

TO LUIS DE CAMOËNS

Without pity, without anger, time abrades
the steel of the heroic swords. You came
home poor and sad to your nostalgic land,
o captain, so that you might die in her
and with her. In her enchanted sand
your Portugal in flower had been lost
and the harsh Spaniard, defeated before,
was threatening her undefended coast.
I want to know if on this side of the last
river you were able humbly to understand
that everything you'd lost, the West, the East,
the sword's steel and the country's flag defeated,
would last (unlike all human things that change)
in the pages of your Portuguese Aeneid.

—s.k.

EL OTRO, EL MISMO

THE SELF AND
THE OTHER

(1964)

UNA BRÚJULA

A Esther Zemborain de Torres

Todas las cosas son palabras del
idioma en que Alguien o Algo, noche y día,
escribe esa infinita algarabía
que es la historia del mundo. En su tropel

pasan Cartago y Roma, yo, tú, él,
mi vida que no entiendo, esta agonía
de ser enigma, azar, criptografía
y toda la discordia de Babel.

Detrás del nombre hay lo que no se nombra;
hoy he sentido gravitar su sombra
en esta aguja azul, lúcida y leve,

que hacia el confín de un mar tiende su empeño,
con algo de reloj visto en un sueño
y algo de ave dormida que se mueve.

COMPASS

For Esther Zemborain de Torres

Every single thing becomes a word
in a language that Someone or Something, night and day,
writes down in a never-ending scribble,
which is the history of the world, embracing

Rome, Carthage, you, me, everyone,
my life, which I do not understand, this anguish
of being enigma, accident, and puzzle,
and all the discordant languages of Babel.

Behind each name lies that which has no name.
Today I felt its nameless shadow tremble
in the blue clarity of the compass needle,

whose rule extends as far as the far seas,
something like a clock glimpsed in a dream
or a bird that stirs suddenly in its sleep.

—A.R.

UNA LLAVE EN SALÓNICA

Abarbanel, Farías o Pinedo,
arrojados de España por impía
persecución, conservan todavía
la llave de una casa de Toledo.

Libres ahora de esperanza y miedo,
miran la llave al declinar el día;
en el bronce hay ayeres, lejanía,
cansado brillo y sufrimiento quedo.

Hoy que su puerta es polvo, el instrumento
es cifra de la diáspora y del viento,
afín a esa otra llave del santuario

que alguien lanzó al azul, cuando el romano
acometió con fuego temerario,
y que en el cielo recibió una mano.

A KEY IN SALONIKA

Abarbanel, Farías or Pinedo,
driven from Spain by the unholy lash
of persecution, still keep close at hand
the key to an old house in Toledo.

Free now as they are of hope or fear,
at day's end they contemplate the key;
within its bronze are distant yesterdays,
a tired luster and a quiet grief.

Now that its door is dust, the instrument
is a cipher of diaspora and wind,
akin to that other sanctuary key

flung into the blue sky when the Romans
attacked it ruthlessly with fire, and
which was received in heaven by a hand.

—S.K.

UN POETA DEL SIGLO XIII

Vuelve a mirar los arduos borradores
de aquel primer soneto innominado,
la página arbitraria en que ha mezclado
tercetos y cuartetos pecadores.

Lima con lenta pluma sus rigores
y se detiene. Acaso le ha llegado
del porvenir y de su horror sagrado
un rumor de remotos ruiseñores.

¿Habrá sentido que no estaba solo
y que el arcano, el increíble Apolo
le había revelado un arquetipo,

un ávido cristal que apresaría
cuanto la noche cierra o abre el día:
dédalo, laberinto, enigma, Edipo?

A POET OF THE THIRTEENTH CENTURY

He looks over the laborious drafts
of that first sonnet (still to be so called),
the random scribbles cluttering the page—
triads, quatrains promiscuously scrawled.

Slowly he smoothes down angularities,
then stops. Has some faint music reached his sense,
notes of far-off nightingales relayed
out of an awesome future ages hence?

Has he realized that he is not alone
and that Apollo, unbelievably arcane,
has made an archetype within him sing—

one crystal-clear and eager to absorb
whatever night conceals or day unveils:
labyrinths, mazes, enigmas, Oedipus King?

—A.S.T.

UN SOLDADO DE URBINA

Sospechándose indigno de otra hazaña
como aquella en el mar, este soldado,
a sórdidos oficios resignado,
erraba oscuro por su dura España.

Para borrar o mitigar la saña
de lo real, buscaba lo soñado
y le dieron un mágico pasado
los ciclos de Rolando y de Bretaña.

Contemplaría, hundido el sol, el ancho
campo en que dura un resplandor de cobre;
se creía acabado, solo y pobre.

sin saber de qué música era dueño;
atravesando el fondo de algún sueño.
por él ya andaban don Quijote y Sancho.

A SOLDIER OF URBINA

Beginning to fear his own unworthiness
for campaigns like the last he fought, at sea,
this soldier, resigning himself to minor duty,
wandered unknown in Spain, his own harsh country.

To get rid of or to mitigate the cruel
weight of reality, he hid his head in dream.
The magic past of Roland and the cycles
of Ancient Britain warmed him, made him welcome.

Sprawled in the sun, he would gaze on the widening
plain, its coppery glow going on and on;
he felt himself at the end, poor and alone,

unaware of the music he was hiding;
plunging deep in a dream of his own,
he came on Sancho and Don Quixote, riding.

—A.R.

EL OTRO

En el primero de sus largos miles
de hexámetros de bronce invoca el griego
a la ardua musa o a un arcano fuego
para cantar la cólera de Aquiles.
Sabía que otro—un Dios—es el que hiere
de brusca luz nuestra labor oscura;
siglos después diría la Escritura
que el Espíritu sopla donde quiere.
La cabal herramienta a su elegido
da el despiadado dios que no se nombra:
a Milton las paredes de la sombra,
el destierro a Cervantes y el olvido.
Suyo es lo que perdura en la memoria
del tiempo secular. Nuestra la escoria.

THE OTHER

In the first line of his long thousands
of bronze hexameters the Greek invokes
an arcane fire or an arduous muse
to help him sing the anger of Achilles.
He knew another—a God—is the one who wounds
our obscure labor with flashes of harsh light;
centuries later the Scriptures would say
that the Spirit blows wherever it might.
It is a pitiless, unnameable God
who gives His chosen one the instrument:
to Milton the enclosing walls of darkness,
exile and oblivion to Cervantes.
In the record of worldly time whatever lasts
belongs to Him. To us, nothing but ash.

—S.K.

UNA ROSA Y MILTON

De las generaciones de las rosas
que en el fondo del tiempo se han perdido
quiero que una se salve del olvido,
una sin marca o signo entre las cosas
que fueron. El destino me depara
este don de nombrar por vez primera
esa flor silenciosa, la postrera
rosa que Milton acercó a su cara,
sin verla. Oh tú bermeja o amarilla
o blanca rosa de un jardín borrado,
deja mágicamente tu pasado
inmemorial y en este verso brilla,
oro, sangre o marfil o tenebrosa
como en sus manos, invisible rosa.

A ROSE AND MILTON

From all the generations of past roses,
Disintegrated in the depths of time,
I want one to be spared oblivion—
One unexceptional rose from all the things
that once existed. Destiny allows me
The privilege of choosing, this first time,
That silent flower, the very final rose
That Milton held before his face, but could
Not see. O rose, vermilion or yellow
Or white, from some obliterated garden,
Your past existence magically lasts
And glows forever in this poetry,
Gold or blood-covered, ivory or shadowed,
As once in Milton's hands, invisible rose.

—A.R.

LECTORES

De aquel hidalgo de cetrina y seca
tez y de heroico afán se conjetura
que, en víspera perpetua de aventura,
no salió nunca de su biblioteca.
La crónica puntual que sus empeños
narra y sus tragicómicos desplantes
fue soñada por él, no por Cervantes,
y no es más que una crónica de sueños.
Tal es también mi suerte. Sé que hay algo
inmortal y esencial que he sepultado
en esa biblioteca del pasado
en que leí la historia del hidalgo.
Las lentas hojas vuelve un niño y grave
sueña con vagas cosas que no sabe.

READERS

Of that gentleman with the sallow, dry complexion
and knightly disposition, they conjecture
that, always on the edge of an adventure,
he never actually left his library.
The precise chronicle of his campaigning
and all its tragicomical reversals
was dreamed by him and not by Cervantes
and is no more than a record of his dreaming.
Such is also my luck. I know there is something
essential and immortal that I have buried
somewhere in that library of the past
in which I read the story of that knight.
The slow leaves now recall a solemn child
who dreams vague things he does not understand.

—A.R.

JUAN, 1, 14

Refieren las historias orientales
la de aquel rey del tiempo, que sujeto
a tedio y esplendor, sale en secreto
y solo, a recorrer los arrabales

y a perderse en la turba de las gentes
de rudas manos y de oscuros nombres;
hoy, como aquel Emir de los Creyentes,
Harún, Dios quiere andar entre los hombres

y nace de una madre, como nacen
los linajes que en polvo se deshacen,
y le será entregado el orbe entero,

aire, agua, pan, mañanas, piedra y lirio,
pero después la sangre del martirio,
el escarnio, los clavos y el madero.

JOHN 1:14

The oriental histories tell a tale
Of a bored king in ancient times who, fraught
With tedium and splendor, went uncaught
And secretly around the slums to sail

Amid the crowds and lose himself in their
Peasant rough hands, their humble obscure names;
Today, like that Muslim Harum, Emeer
Of the true faithful, God decides to claim

His place on earth, born of a mother in
A lineage that will dissolve in bones,
And the whole world will have its origin

With him: air, water, bread, mornings, stones,
Lily. But soon the blood of martydom,
The curse, the heavy spikes, the beams. Then numb.

— W.B.

EL DESPERTAR

Entra la luz y asciendo torpemente
de los sueños al sueño compartido
y las cosas recobran su debido
y esperado lugar y en el presente
converge abrumador y vasto el vago
ayer: las seculares migraciones
del pájaro y del hombre, las legiones
que el hierro destrozó, Roma y Cartago.
Vuelve también la cotidiana historia:
mi voz, mi rostro, mi temor, mi suerte.
¡Ah, si aquel otro despertar, la muerte,
me deparara un tiempo sin memoria
de mi nombre y de todo lo que he sido!
¡Ah, si en esa mañana hubiera olvido!

WAKING UP

Daylight leaks in, and sluggishly I surface
from my own dreams into the common dream
and things assume again their proper places
and their accustomed shapes. Into this present
the Past intrudes, in all its dizzying range—
the centuries-old habits of migration
in birds and men, the armies in their legions
all fallen to the sword, and Rome and Carthage.
The trappings of my day also come back:
my voice, my face, my nervousness, my luck.
If only Death, that other waking-up,
would grant me a time free of all memory
of my own name and all that I have been!
If only morning meant oblivion!

— A.R.

A QUIEN YA NO ES JOVEN

Ya puedes ver el trágico escenario
y cada cosa en el lugar debido;
la espada y la ceniza para Dido
y la moneda para Belisario.

¿A qué sigues buscando en el brumoso
bronce de los hexámetros la guerra
si están aquí los siete pies de tierra,
la brusca sangre y el abierto foso?

Aquí te acecha el insondable espejo
que soñará y olvidará el reflejo
de tus postrimerías y agonías.

Ya te cerca lo último. Es la casa
donde tu lenta y breve tarde pasa
y la calle que ves todos los días.

TO ONE NO LONGER YOUNG

Already you can see the tragic setting
And each thing there in its appointed place;
The broadsword and the ash destined for Dido,
The coin ready for Belisarius.

Why do you go on searching in the hazy
Bronze of old hexameters for war
When seven feet of ground wait for you here,
The sudden rush of blood, the open grave?

Here watching you is the inscrutable glass
that will dream up and then forget the face
Of all your dwindling days, your agonies.

The last one now draws near. It is the house
In which your slow, brief evening comes to pass
And the street that you look at every day.

—A.R.

ALEXANDER SELKIRK

Sueño que el mar, el mar aquel, me encierra
y del sueño me salvan las campanas
de Dios, que santifican las mañanas
de estos íntimos campos de Inglaterra.

Cinco años padecí mirando eternas
cosas de soledad y de infinito,
que ahora son esa historia que repito,
ya como una obsesión, en las tabernas.

Dios me ha devuelto al mundo de los hombres,
a espejos, puertas, números y nombres,
y ya no soy aquel que eternamente

miraba el mar y su profunda estepa
¿y cómo haré para que ese otro sepa
que estoy aquí, salvado, entre mi gente?

ALEXANDER SELKIRK

I dream the sea, that sea, surrounding me,
And from the dream I'm rescued by the bells
Of God, which bless and sanctify the mornings
Of these domesticated English fields.

Five years I suffered, looking at eternal
Images of infinity and solitude,
Which have become that story I repeat
Now, like an obsession, in the pubs.

God has returned me to the world of men,
To mirrors and doors and numbers and names,
And I am no longer he who eternally

Looked at the sea and its deep barren plain.
But now what shall I do so it may find
That I am here, and safe, among my kind?

         —S.K.

ODISEA, LIBRO VIGÉSIMO TERCERO

Ya la espada de hierro ha ejecutado
la debida labor de la venganza;
ya los ásperos dardos y la lanza
la sangre del perverso han prodigado.

A despecho de un dios y de sus mares
a su reino y su reina ha vuelto Ulises,
a despecho de un dios y de los grises
vientos y del estrépito de Ares.

Ya en el amor del compartido lecho
duerme la clara reina sobre el pecho
de su rey pero ¿dónde está aquel hombre

que en los días y noches del destierro
erraba por el mundo como un perro
y decía que Nadie era su nombre?

ODYSSEY, BOOK TWENTY-THREE

Now has the rapier of iron wrought
The work of justice, and revenge is done.
Now spear and arrows, pitiless every one,
Have made the blood of insolence run out.

For all a god and all his seas could do
Ulysses has returned to realm and queen.
For all a god could do, and the gray-green
Gales and Ares' murderous hullabaloo.

Now in the love of their own bridal bed
The shining queen has fallen asleep, her head
Upon her king's breast. Where is that man now

Who in his exile wandered night and day
Over the world like a wild dog, and would say
His name was No One, No One, anyhow?

—R.F.

ÉL

Los ojos de tu carne ven el brillo
del insufrible sol, tu carne toca
polvo disperso o apretada roca;
Él es la luz, lo negro y lo amarillo.
Es y los ve. Desde incesantes ojos
te mira y es los ojos que un reflejo
indagan y los ojos del espejo,
las negras hidras y los tigres rojos.
No le basta crear. Es cada una
de las criaturas de Su extraño mundo:
las porfiadas raíces del profundo
cedro y las mutaciones de la luna.
Me llamaban Caín. Por mí el Eterno
sabe el sabor del fuego del infierno.

HE

Your fleshly eyes cannot escape the glare
of the insufferable sun, your flesh can touch
nothing but scattered dust and crushed rock;
He is the light, the yellow and the black.
He is and He sees. With His relentless gaze
He watches you and is the eyes inspecting
a reflection and the eyes in the mirror,
eyes of the red tigers and the black snakes.
For Him, creation is not enough. He must
be every single creature in His strange world:
the stubborn roots that reach deep underneath
the cedar and the phases of the moon.
They called me Cain. Through me the Eternal One
can taste the fire of hell upon His tongue.

—S.K.

A UN POETA MENOR DE 1899

Dejar un verso para la hora triste
que en el confín del día nos acecha,
ligar tu nombre a su doliente fecha
de oro y de vaga sombra. Eso quisiste.
¡Con qué pasión, al declinar el día,
trabajarías el extraño verso
que, hasta la dispersión del universo,
la hora de extraño azul confirmaría!
No sé si lo lograste ni siquiera,
vago hermano mayor, si has existido,
pero estoy solo y quiero que el olvido
restituya a los días tu ligera
sombra para este ya cansado alarde
de unas palabras en que esté la tarde.

TO A MINOR POET OF 1899

To leave a verse concerning the sad hour
That awaits us at the limit of the day,
To bind your name to its sorrowful date
Of gold and of vague shade. That's what you wanted.
With what passion as the day drew to its close
You labored on and on at the strange verse
That, until the universe disperses,
Would confirm the hour of the strange blue!
I do not know if ever you succeeded
Nor, vague elder brother, if you existed,
But I am alone and want oblivion
To restore your fleeting shade to the days
In the supreme already worn-out effort
Of words wherein the evening may yet be.

—C.T.

TEXAS

Aquí también. Aquí, como en el otro
confín del continente, el infinito
campo en que muere solitario el grito;
aquí también el indio, el lazo, el potro.
Aquí también el pájaro secreto
que sobre los fragores de la historia
canta para una tarde y su memoria;
aquí también el místico alfabeto
de los astros, que hoy dictan a mi cálamo
nombres que el incesante laberinto
de los días no arrastra: San Jacinto
y esas otras Termópilas, el Alamo.
Aquí también esa desconocida
y ansiosa y breve cosa que es la vida.

TEXAS

Here too. Here as at the other edge
Of the hemisphere, an endless plain
Where a man's cry dies a lonely death.
Here too the Indian, the lasso, the wild horse.
Here too the bird that never shows itself,
That sings for the memory of one evening
Over the rumblings of history;
Here too the mystic alphabet of stars
Leading my pen over the page to names
Not swept aside in the continual
Labyrinth of days: San Jacinto
And that other Thermopylae, the Alamo.
Here too the never understood,
Anxious, and brief affair that is life.

—M.S.

COMPOSICIÓN ESCRITA EN UN
EJEMPLAR DE LA GESTA DE *BEOWULF*

A veces me pregunto qué razones
me mueven a estudiar sin esperanza
de precisión, mientras mi noche avanza,
la lengua de los ásperos sajones.
Gastada por los años la memoria
deja caer la en vano repetida
palabra y es así como mi vida
teje y desteje su cansada historia.
Será (me digo entonces) que de un modo
secreto y suficiente el alma sabe
que es inmortal y que su vasto y grave
círculo abarca todo y puede todo.
Más allá de este afán y de este verso
me aguarda inagotable el universo.

POEM WRITTEN IN A
COPY OF *BEOWULF*

At various times I have asked myself what reasons
moved me to study while my night came down,
without particular hope of satisfaction,
the language of the blunt-tongued Anglo-Saxons.
Used up by the years my memory
loses its grip on words that I have vainly
repeated and repeated. My life in the same way
weaves and unweaves its weary history.
Then I tell myself: it must be that the soul
has some secret sufficient way of knowing
that it is immortal, that its vast encompassing
circle can take in all, accomplish all.
Beyond my anxiety and beyond this writing
the universe waits, inexhaustible, inviting.

—A.R.

A UNA ESPADA EN YORK MINSTER

En su hierro perdura el hombre fuerte,
hoy polvo de planeta, que en las guerras
de ásperos mares y arrasadas tierras
lo esgrimió, vano al fin, contra la muerte.

Vana también la muerte. Aquí está el hombre
blanco y feral que de Noruega vino,
urgido por el épico destino;
su espada es hoy su símbolo y su nombre.

Pese a la larga muerte y su destierro,
la mano atroz sigue oprimiendo el hierro
y soy sombra en la sombra ante el guerrero

cuya sombra está aquí. Soy un instante
y el instante ceniza, no diamante,
y sólo lo pasado es verdadero.

TO A SWORD AT YORK MINSTER

The strong man in its iron still lives on,
Now changed to planet dust who once in wars
On the rough seas and in the flattened fields
Brandished it, at last in vain, at death.

Vain, even death itself. Here is the man
Who white and feral out of Norway came
Urged forward by an epic destiny;
His sword is now his image and his name.

In spite of his long death and his exile,
The inhuman hand clutches the iron still.
And I am shade within a shade before him

Whose shade is here. I am a single instant
And the instant ashes and not diamond,
And only what is past is what is real.

— C.T.

SNORRI STURLUSON
(1179–1241)

Tú que legaste una mitología
de hielo y fuego a la filial memoria,
tú, que fijaste la violenta gloria
de tu estirpe de acero y de osadía,

sentiste con asombro en una tarde
de espadas que tu triste carne humana
temblaba. En esa tarde sin mañana
te fue dado saber que eras cobarde.

En la noche de Islandia, la salobre
borrasca mueve el mar. Está cercada
tu casa. Has bebido hasta las heces

el deshonor inolvidable. Sobre
tu pálida cabeza cae la espada
como en tu libro cayó tantas veces.

SNORRI STURLUSON
(1179–1241)

You who bequeathed us a mythology
of ice and fire and filial memory,
you, who fixed in words the violent glory
of your long lineage of steel and courage,

felt with astonishment one fateful dusk
under the sword the trembling of your sad
human flesh. On that night with no tomorrow
it dawned on you that you were a coward.

In the Icelandic dark the salty storm
tosses the ocean waves. Your house is fenced.
You have drunk down to the bitter dregs

the unforgettable dishonor. On
your pale head the sword keeps coming down
as in your book it fell time and again.

—S.K.

A CARLOS XII

Viking de las estepas, Carlos Doce
de Suecia, que cumpliste aquel camino
del Septentrión al Sur de tu divino
antecesor Odín, fueron tu goce
los trabajos que mueven la memoria
de los hombres al canto, la batalla
mortal, el duro horror de la metralla,
la firme espada y la sangrienta gloria.
Supiste que vencer o ser vencido
son caras de un Azar indiferente,
que no hay otra virtud que ser valiente
y que el mármol, al fin, será el olvido.
Ardes glacial, más solo que el desierto;
nadie llegó a tu alma y ya estás muerto.

TO CHARLES XII

Viking of the steppes, Charles the Twelfth
of Sweden, who marched that whole long road
of the Great Bear to the South of your divine
ancestor Odin, what gave you pleasure were
the efforts so great they moved men's memory
to epic verse and song, the deadly battles,
hard horror of cannon fire, the steel
unyielding sword and the bloody glory.
You knew that to prevail or to be conquered
were two sides of the same indifferent Coin,
that to be brave was the only virtue
and one's cold monument will be oblivion.
You burn like ice, more desolate than the desert;
no one could touch your soul, and now you're gone.

— S.K.

EMANUEL SWEDENBORG

Más alto que los otros, caminaba
aquel hombre lejano entre los hombres;
apenas si llamaba por sus nombres
secretos a los ángeles. Miraba
lo que no ven los ojos terrenales:
la ardiente geometría, el cristalino
edificio de Dios y el remolino
sórdido de los goces infernales.
Sabía que la Gloria y el Averno
en tu alma están y sus mitologías;
sabía, como el griego, que los días
del tiempo son espejos del Eterno.
En árido latín fue registrando
últimas cosas sin por qué ni cuándo.

EMANUEL SWEDENBORG

He loomed above the others when he walked,
That man who was remote among good men;
By secret names he called them when he talked
To angels. When he gazed beyond his pen,
He saw what earthly eyes can never look upon:
Burning geometry, the crystal dome
Of God, and the disgusting whirlwind home
Of those infernal joys nourished each dawn.
He knew that Glory and the gate of Hell
And their mythologies live in your soul.
He knew, like Heraclitus, that one day
Of time's a mirror of eternity,
And in dry Latin found the final role
Of things whose why or when he wouldn't tell.

— W.B.

JONATHAN EDWARDS
(1703-1785)

Lejos de la ciudad, lejos del foro
clamoroso y del tiempo, que es mudanza,
Edwards, eterno ya, sueña y avanza
a la sombra de árboles de oro.
Hoy es mañana y es ayer. No hay una
cosa de Dios en el sereno ambiente
que no lo exalte misteriosamente,
el oro de la tarde o de la luna.
Piensa feliz que el mundo es un eterno
instrumento de ira y que el ansiado
cielo para unos pocos fue creado
y casi para todos el infierno.
En el centro puntual de la maraña
hay otro prisionero, Dios, la Araña.

JONATHAN EDWARDS
(1703–1785)

Far from the marketplace, the city's roar,
from mutating time, eternal now at last,
Jonathan Edwards dreams and makes his way
through shadows trees of golden foliage cast.
Today is tomorrow and yesterday.
In God's cloudless cosmos all things hold
Him in exaltation mysteriously,
the gold of evening and the moon of gold.
Blissful, he thinks the world an everlasting
instrument of God's wrath, the heaven all seek
reserved for the happy few whom God acquits,
the lot of everyone else the fires of hell.
In the very center of the tangled web
another prisoner, God the Spider, sits.

—A.S.T.

EMERSON

Ese alto caballero americano
cierra el volumen de Montaigne y sale
en busca de otro goce que no vale
menos, la tarde que ya exalta el llano.
Hacia el hondo poniente y su declive,
hacia el confín que ese poniente dora,
camina por los campos como ahora
por la memoria de quien esto escribe.
Piensa: Leí los libros esenciales
y otros compuse que el oscuro olvido
no ha de borrar. Un dios me ha concedido
lo que es dado saber a los mortales.
Por todo el continente anda mi nombre;
no he vivido. Quisiera ser otro hombre.

EMERSON

Closing the heavy volume of Montaigne,
The tall New Englander goes out
Into an evening which exalts the fields.
It is a pleasure worth no less than reading.
He walks toward the final sloping of the sun,
Toward the landscape's gilded edge;
He moves through darkening fields as he moves now
Through the memory of the one who writes this down.
He thinks: I have read the essential books
And written others which oblivion
Will not efface. I have been allowed
That which is given mortal man to know.
The whole continent knows my name.
I have not lived. I want to be someone else.

—M.S.

EDGAR ALLAN POE

Pompas del mármol, negra anatomía
que ultrajan los gusanos sepulcrales,
del triunfo de la muerte los glaciales
símbolos congregó. No los temía.

Temía la otra sombra, la amorosa,
las comunes venturas de la gente;
no lo cegó el metal resplandeciente
ni el mármol sepulcral sino la rosa.

Como del otro lado del espejo
se entregó solitario a su complejo
destino de inventor de pesadillas.

Quizá, del otro lado de la muerte,
siga erigiendo solitario y fuerte
espléndidas y atroces maravillas.

EDGAR ALLAN POE

Pageants of marble, black anatomy
violated by worms inside the grave,
he gathered icy symbols of death's victory.
But of those things he was not afraid.

What he feared was another darkness, love,
the ordinary happiness of people;
what blinded him was not the shiny metal
nor marble tombstones but the simple rose.

As if from the other side of the mirror
he was delivered alone into his complex
destiny: to be an inventor of nightmares.

Perhaps now from the other side of death
he keeps constructing, strong and all alone,
magnificent and horrifying wonders.

— S.K.

CAMDEN, 1892

El olor del café y de los periódicos.
El domingo y su tedio. La mañana
y en la entrevista página esa vana
publicación de versos alegóricos
de un colega feliz. El hombre viejo
está postrado y blanco en su decente
habitación de pobre. Ociosamente
mira su cara en el cansado espejo.
Piensa, ya sin asombro, que esa cara
es él. La distraída mano toca
la turbia barba y la saqueada boca.
No está lejos el fin. Su voz declara:
Casi no soy, pero mis versos ritman
la vida y su esplendor. Yo fui Walt Whitman.

CAMDEN, 1892

The smell of coffee and the newspapers.
Sunday and its lassitudes. The morning,
and on the adjoining page, that vanity—
the publication of allegorical verses
by a fortunate fellow poet. The old man
lies on a white bed in his sober room,
a poor man's habitation. Languidly
he gazes at his face in the worn mirror.
He thinks, beyond astonishment now: *that man
is me*, and absentmindedly his hand
touches the unkempt beard and the worn-out mouth.
The end is close. He mutters to himself:
I am almost dead, but still my poems retain
life and its wonders. I was once Walt Whitman.

—A.R.

PARÍS, 1856

La larga postración lo ha acostumbrado
a anticipar la muerte. Le daría
miedo salir al clamoroso día
y andar entre los hombres. Derribado,
Enrique Heine piensa en aquel río,
el tiempo, que lo aleja lentamente
de esa larga penumbra y del doliente
destino de ser hombre y ser judío.
Piensa en las delicadas melodías
cuyo instrumento fue, pero bien sabe
que el trino no es del árbol ni del ave
sino del tiempo y de sus vagos días.
No han de salvarte, no, tus ruiseñores,
tus noches de oro y tus cantadas flores.

PARIS, 1856

The long prostration has accustomed him
To anticipate his death. His concrete dread
Is going out of doors into the whim
Of day to walk about with friends. Ravaged,
Heinrich Heine thinks about that river
Of time that slowly moves away into
That lingering penumbra and the bitter
Hurt destiny of being a man and Jew.
He thinks about exquisite melodies
Whose instrument he was, and yet he knows
The trilling doesn't come from trees or birds
But time and from the days' slim vagaries.
And yet your nightingales won't save you, no,
Nor nights of gold and flowers sung in your words.

— W.B.

RAFAEL CANSINOS-ASSÉNS

La imagen de aquel pueblo lapidado
y execrado, inmortal en su agonía,
en las negras vigilias lo atraía
con una suerte de terror sagrado.
Bebió como quien bebe un hondo vino
los Psalmos y el Cantar de la Escritura
y sintió que era suya esa dulzura
y sintió que era suyo aquel destino.
Lo llamaba Israel. Íntimamente
la oyó Cansinos como oyó el profeta
en la secreta cumbre la secreta
voz del Señor desde la zarza ardiente.
Acompáñeme siempre su memoria;
las otras cosas las dirá la gloria.

RAFAEL CANSINOS-ASSÉNS

The image of that place reduced to rubble
and vilified, an immortal desecration
haunted him in the darkest of his vigils
with all the fateful feel of holy dread.
As one might taste the subtlest of wines
he read aloud the Psalms and the Song of Songs
and felt their sweetness as his own sweetness,
and knew their destiny to be his own.
He spoke of it as Israel. Deeply, deeply,
Cansinos heard its voice, as the prophet heard
on the secret heights the voice of God himself
speaking from within the burning bush.
May my memory of him remain a constant presence.
Everything else will guarantee his glory.

—A.R.

LOS ENIGMAS

Yo que soy el que ahora está cantando
seré mañana el misterioso, el muerto,
el morador de un mágico y desierto
orbe sin antes ni después ni cuándo.
Así afirma la mística. Me creo
indigno del Infierno o de la Gloria,
pero nada predigo. Nuestra historia
cambia como las formas de Proteo.
¿Qué errante laberinto, qué blancura
ciega de resplandor será mi suerte,
cuando me entregue el fin de esta aventura
la curiosa experiencia de la muerte?
Quiero beber su cristalino Olvido,
ser para siempre; pero no haber sido.

THE ENIGMAS

I who am singing these lines today
Will be tomorrow the enigmatic corpse
Who dwells in a realm, magical and barren,
Without a before or an after or a when.
So say the mystics. I say I believe
Myself undeserving of Heaven or of Hell,
But make no predictions. Each man's tale
Shifts like the watery forms of Proteus.
What errant labyrinth, what blinding flash
Of splendor and glory shall become my fate
When the end of this adventure presents me with
The curious experience of death?
I want to drink its crystal-pure oblivion,
To be forever; but never to have been.

—J.U.

EL INSTANTE

¿Dónde estarán los siglos, dónde el sueño
de espadas que los tártaros soñaron,
dónde los fuertes muros que allanaron,
dónde el Árbol de Adán y el otro Leño?
El presente está solo. La memoria
erige el tiempo. Sucesión y engaño
es la rutina del reloj. El año
no es menos vano que la vana historia.
Entre el alba y la noche hay un abismo
de agonías, de luces, de cuidados;
el rostro que se mira en los gastados
espejos de la noche no es el mismo.
El hoy fugaz es tenue y es eterno;
otro Cielo no esperes, ni otro Infierno.

THE INSTANT

Where are the centuries, where is the dream
of sword-strife that the Tartars entertained,
where are the massive ramparts that they flattened?
Where is the wood of the Cross, the Tree of Adam?
The present is singular. It is memory
that sets up time. Both succession and error
come with the routine of the clock. A year
is no less vanity than is history.
Between dawn and nightfall is an abyss
of agonies, felicities, and cares.
The face that looks back from the wasted mirrors,
the mirrors of night, is not the same face.
The fleeting day is frail and is eternal:
expect no other Heaven, no other Hell.

—A.R.

SONETO DEL VINO

¿En qué reino, en qué siglo, bajo qué silenciosa
conjunción de los astros, en qué secreto día
que el mármol no ha salvado, surgió la valerosa
y singular idea de inventar la alegría?
Con otoños de oro la inventaron. El vino
fluye rojo a lo largo de las generaciones
como el río del tiempo y en el arduo camino
nos prodiga su música, su fuego y sus leones.
En la noche del júbilo o en la jornada adversa
exalta la alegría o mitiga el espanto
y el ditirambo nuevo que este día le canto
otrora lo cantaron el árabe y el persa.
Vino, enséñame el arte de ver mi propia historia
como si ésta ya fuera ceniza en la memoria.

WINE SONNET

What realm, what age, what century, what silent
alignment of the stars, what secret day
unmarked in marble gave rise to the brave
and singular notion of inventing joy?
It was invented with the gold of autumns. Wine
flows red down through the generations like
the river of time and on the hard road
it graces us with music, fire and lions.
In jubilant nights or at the end of a dark day
it cheers us on or mitigates our fear
and the song of praise I sing for it today
the Arab and the Persian sang before.
Wine, teach me the art of seeing my own past
as if it were already memory's ash.

—S.K.

1964

I

Ya no es mágico el mundo. Te han dejado.
Ya no compartirás la clara luna
ni los lentos jardines. Ya no hay una
luna que no sea espejo del pasado,
cristal de soledad, sol de agonías.
Adiós las mutuas manos y las sienes
que acercaba el amor. Hoy sólo tienes
la fiel memoria y los desiertos días.
Nadie pierde (repites vanamente)
sino lo que no tiene y no ha tenido
nunca, pero no basta ser valiente
para aprender el arte del olvido.
Un símbolo, una rosa, te desgarra
y te puede matar una guitarra.

1964

I

It is not magic now, the world. Alone,
you will not share the clarity of moonlight
or the placid gardens. Now there will be no moon
that is not a reflection of the past,
mirror of solitude, a sun of sorrow.
Goodbye now to the touch of hands and bodies
that love brought close together. Now you have only
your loyal memories and the empty days.
We only lose (you vainly tell yourself)
what we do not have, what we have never had.
But, to learn the fine art of forgetting,
it is not enough to put on a brave face.
Some sign—a rose—can tear the heart from you
and a chord on a guitar can do you in.

II

Ya no seré feliz. Tal vez no importa.
Hay tantas otras cosas en el mundo;
un instante cualquiera es más profundo
y diverso que el mar. La vida es corta
y aunque las horas son tan largas, una
oscura maravilla nos acecha,
la muerte, ese otro mar, esa otra flecha
que nos libra del sol y de la luna
y del amor. La dicha que me diste
y me quitaste debe ser borrada;
lo que era todo tiene que ser nada.
Sólo me queda el goce de estar triste.
esa vana costumbre que me inclina
al Sur, a cierta puerta, a cierta esquina.

II

I will not be happy now. It may not matter.
There are so many more things in the world.
Any random instant is as crowded
and varied as the sea. A life is brief,
and though the hours seem long, there is another
dark mystery that lies in wait for us
—death, that other sea, that other arrow
that frees us from the sun, the moon, and love.
The happiness you gave me once and later
took back from me will be obliterated.
That which was everything must turn to nothing.
I only keep the taste of my own sadness
and a vain urge that turns me to the Southside,
to a certain corner there, a certain door.

— A.R.

A QUIEN ESTÁ LEYÉNDOME

Eres invulnerable. ¿No te han dado
los númenes que rigen tu destino
certidumbre de polvo? ¿No es acaso
tu irreversible tiempo el de aquel río
en cuyo espejo Heráclito vio el símbolo
de su fugacidad? Te espera el mármol
que no leerás. En él ya están escritos
la fecha, la ciudad y el epitafio.
Sueños del tiempo son también los otros,
no firme bronce ni acendrado oro;
el universo es, como tú, Proteo.
Sombra, irás a la sombra que te aguarda
fatal en el confín de tu jornada;
piensa que de algún modo ya estás muerto.

TO WHOEVER IS READING ME

You are invulnerable. Have they not granted you,
those powers that preordain your destiny,
the certainty of dust? Is not your time
as irreversible as that same river
where Heraclitus, mirrored, saw the symbol
of fleeting life? A marble slab awaits you
which you will not read—on it, already written,
the date, the city, and the epitaph.
Other men too are only dreams of time,
not indestructible bronze or burnished gold;
the universe is, like you, a Proteus.
Dark, you will enter the darkness that awaits you,
doomed to the limits of your traveled time.
Know that in some sense you are already dead.

—A.R.

EVERNESS

Sólo una cosa no hay. Es el olvido.
Dios, que salva el metal, salva la escoria
y cifra en Su profética memoria
las lunas que serán y las que han sido.

Ya todo está. Los miles de reflejos
que entre los dos crepúsculos del día
tu rostro fue dejando en los espejos
y los que irá dejando todavía.

Y todo es una parte del diverso
cristal de esa memoria, el universo;
no tienen fin sus arduos corredores

y las puertas se cierran a tu paso;
sólo del otro lado del ocaso
verás los Arquetipos y Esplendores.

EVERNESS

One thing alone does not exist—oblivion.
God, who saves the metal, saves the dross
and stores in his prophetic memory
moons that have still to come, moons that have shone.

Everything is there. The thousands of reflections
which between the dawn and the twilight
your face has left behind in many mirrors
and those faces it will go on leaving yet.

And everything is part of that diverse
and mirroring memory, the universe;
there is no end to its exigent corridors

and the doors that close behind you as you go;
only the far side of the sunset's glow
will show you at last the Archetypes and Splendors.

—A.R.

EWIGKEIT

Torne en mi boca el verso castellano
a decir lo que siempre está diciendo
desde el latín de Séneca: el horrendo
dictamen de que todo es del gusano.

Torne a cantar la pálida ceniza,
los fastos de la muerte y la victoria
de esa reina retórica que pisa
los estandartes de la vanagloria.

No así. Lo que mi barro ha bendecido
no lo voy a negar como un cobarde.
Sé que una cosa no hay. Es el olvido;

sé que en la eternidad perdura y arde
lo mucho y lo precioso que he perdido:
esa fragua, esa luna y esa tarde.

EWIGKEIT

Let the line of the Spanish poem come
back to my lips to say what it has said
ever since Seneca first said it in Latin:
the horrid judgment that we are food for worms.

Let the pale ashes return to sing their song,
the chronicles of death and the victory
of that rhetorical queen who treads upon
the banners of our pride and vanity.

But no. Whatever has blessed this clay of mine
I'm not going to deny as a coward would.
I know one thing does not exist: forgetting;

I know that all the precious things I've lost
endure eternally, to be and burn:
that blacksmith's forge, that evening and that moon.

                                                    — S.K.

EDIPO Y EL ENIGMA

Cuadrúpedo en la aurora, alto en el día
y con tres pies errando por el vano
ámbito de la tarde, así veía
la eterna esfinge a su inconstante hermano,

el hombre, y con la tarde un hombre vino
que descifró aterrado en el espejo
de la monstruosa imagen, el reflejo
de su declinación y su destino.

Somos Edipo y de un eterno modo
la larga y triple bestia somos, todo
lo que seremos y lo que hemos sido.

Nos aniquilaría ver la ingente
forma de nuestro ser; piadosamente
Dios nos depara sucesión y olvido.

OEDIPUS AND THE ENIGMA

Four-footed at dawn, in the daytime tall,
and wandering three-legged down the hollow
reaches of evening: thus did the sphinx,
the eternal one, regard his restless fellow,

mankind; and at evening came a man
who, terror-struck, discovered as in a mirror
his own decline set forth in the monstrous image,
his destiny, and felt a chill of terror.

We are Oedipus and everlastingly
we are the long tripartite beast; we are
all that we were and will be, nothing less.

It would destroy us to look steadily
at our full being. Mercifully God grants us
the ticking of the clock, forgetfulness.

—A.S.T.

SPINOZA

Las traslúcidas manos del judío
labran en la penumbra los cristales
y la tarde que muere es miedo y frío.
(Las tardes a las tardes son iguales.)

Las manos y el espacio de jacinto
que palidece en el confín del Ghetto
casi no existen para el hombre quieto
que está soñando un claro laberinto.

No lo turba la fama, ese reflejo
de sueños en el sueño de otro espejo,
ni el temeroso amor de las doncellas.

Libre de la metáfora y del mito
labra un arduo cristal: el infinito
mapa de Aquél que es todas Sus estrellas.

SPINOZA

Here in the twilight the translucent hands
Of the Jew polishing the crystal glass.
The dying afternoon is cold with bands
Of fear. Each day the afternoons all pass

The same. The hands and space of hyacinth
Paling in the confines of the ghetto walls
Barely exist for the quiet man who stalls
There, dreaming up a brilliant labyrinth.

Fame doesn't trouble him (that reflection of
Dreams in the dream of another mirror), nor love,
The timid love of women. Gone the bars,

He's free, from metaphor and myth, to sit
Polishing a stubborn lens: the infinite
Map of the One who now is all His stars.

— W.B.

ADAM CAST FORTH

¿Hubo un Jardín o fue el Jardín un sueño?
Lento en la vaga luz, me he preguntado.
casi como un consuelo, si el pasado
de que este Adán, hoy mísero, era dueño,

no fue sino una mágica impostura
de aquel Dios que soñé. Ya es impreciso
en la memoria el claro Paraíso,
pero yo sé que existe y que perdura,

aunque no para mí. La terca tierra
es mi castigo y la incestuosa guerra
de Caínes y Abeles y su cría.

Y, sin embargo, es mucho haber amado,
haber sido feliz, haber tocado
el viviente Jardín, siquiera un día.

ADAM CAST FORTH

The Garden—was it real or was it dream?
Slow in the hazy light, I have been asking,
Almost as a comfort, if the past
Belonging to this now unhappy Adam

Was nothing but a magic fantasy
Of that God I dreamed. Now it is imprecise
In memory, that lucid paradise,
But I know it exists and will persist

Though not for me. The unforgiving earth
Is my affliction, and the incestuous wars
Of Cains and Abels and their progeny.

Nevertheless, it means much to have loved,
To have been happy, to have laid my hand on
The living Garden, even for one day.

—A.R.

EL SUEÑO

Si el sueño fuera (como dicen) una
tregua, un puro reposo de la mente,
¿por qué, si te despiertan bruscamente,
sientes que te han robado una fortuna?
¿Por qué es tan triste madrugar? La hora
nos despoja de un don inconcebible,
tan íntimo que sólo es traducible
en un sopor que la vigilia dora
de sueños, que bien pueden ser reflejos
truncos de los tesoros de la sombra,
de un orbe intemporal que no se nombra
y que el día deforma en sus espejos.
¿Quién serás esta noche en el oscuro
sueño, del otro lado de su muro?

DREAM

If dreaming really were a kind of truce
(as people claim), a sheer repose of mind,
why then if you should waken up abruptly,
do you feel that something has been stolen from you?
Why should it be so sad, the early morning?
It robs us of an inconceivable gift,
so intimate it is only knowable
in a trance which the nightwatch gilds with dreams,
dreams that might very well be reflections,
fragments from the treasure-house of darkness,
from the timeless sphere that does not have a name,
and that the day distorts in its mirrors.
Who will you be tonight in your dreamfall
into the dark, on the other side of the wall?

— A.R.

JUNÍN

Soy, pero soy también el otro, el muerto,
el otro de mi sangre y de mi nombre;
soy un vago señor y soy el hombre
que detuvo las lanzas del desierto.
Vuelvo a Junín, donde no estuve nunca,
a tu Junín, abuelo Borges. ¿Me oyes,
sombra o ceniza última, o desoyes
en tu sueño de bronce esta voz trunca?
Acaso buscas por mis vanos ojos
el épico Junín de tus soldados,
el árbol que plantaste, los cercados
y en el confín la tribu y los despojos.
Te imagino severo, un poco triste.
Quién me dirá cómo eras y quién fuiste.

Junín, 1966.

JUNÍN

I am, but am also the other one, now dead,
the other of my blood and with my name;
I'm some kind of gentleman and am the man
who stopped the lances in the desert wastes.
I come home to Junín, where I never was,
to your Junín, Grandfather Borges. Do you hear,
ultimate shade or ashes, or not hear
in your bronze dream this stunted voice of mine?
Perhaps you're seeking through my own vain eyes
the epic Junín of your troops, the trees
you planted, the fences and walls you raised,
and on that ground the tribe and its remains.
I imagine you a little sad, severe.
Who will tell me how and who you were?

—S.K.

UN SOLDADO DE LEE
(1862)

Lo ha alcanzado una bala en la ribera
de una clara corriente cuyo nombre
ignora. Cae de boca. (Es verdadera
la historia y más de un hombre fue aquel hombre.)
El aire de oro mueve las ociosas
hojas de los pinares. La paciente
hormiga escala el rostro indiferente.
Sube el sol. Ya han cambiado muchas cosas
y cambiarán sin término hasta cierto
día del porvenir en que te canto
a ti que, sin la dádiva del llanto,
caíste como un hombre muerto.
No hay un mármol que guarde tu memoria;
seis pies de tierra son tu oscura gloria.

ONE OF LEE'S SOLDIERS
(1862)

A bullet has caught him on the bank of a river
with a clear current and a name he never
knew. He falls face down. (This is a true
story and about more than just one man.)
A golden breeze rustles the lazy green
pine branches. An ant with infinite patience
is climbing the slope of his indifferent face.
The sun comes up. A lot of things have changed
and will continue changing endlessly
until some future day when I will sing
to you that, lacking the gift of another's grief,
you fell as one who'd already gone down.
No marble statue guards your memory;
your obscure heaven is six feet of ground.

—S.K.

EL MAR

Antes que el sueño (o el terror) tejiera
mitologías y cosmogonías,
antes que el tiempo se acuñara en días,
el mar, el siempre mar, ya estaba y era.
¿Quién es el mar? ¿Quién es aquel violento
y antiguo ser que roe los pilares
de la tierra y es uno y muchos mares
y abismo y resplandor y azar y viento?
Quien lo mira lo ve por vez primera,
siempre. Con el asombro que las cosas
elementales dejan, las hermosas
tardes, la luna, el fuego de una hoguera.
¿Quién es el mar, quién soy? Lo sabré el día
ulterior que sucede a la agonía.

THE SEA

Before our human dream (or terror) wove
Mythologies, cosmogonies, and love,
Before time coined its substance into days,
The sea, the always sea, existed: was.
Who is the sea? Who is that violent being,
Violent and ancient, who gnaws the foundations
Of earth? He is both one and many oceans;
He is abyss and splendor, chance and wind.
Who looks on the sea, sees it the first time,
Every time, with the wonder distilled
From elementary things—from beautiful
Evenings, the moon, the leap of a bonfire.
Who is the sea, and who am I? The day
That follows my last agony shall say.

—J.U.

UNA MAÑANA DE 1649

Carlos avanza entre su pueblo. Mira
a izquierda y a derecha. Ha rechazado
los brazos de la escolta. Liberado
de la necesidad de la mentira,

sabe que hoy va a la muerte, no al olvido,
y que es un rey. La ejecución lo espera;
la mañana es atroz y verdadera.
No hay temor en su carne. Siempre ha sido,

a fuer de buen tahúr, indiferente.
Ha apurado la vida hasta las heces;
ahora está solo entre la armada gente.

No lo infama el patíbulo. Los jueces
no son el Juez. Saluda levemente
y sonríe. Lo ha hecho tantas veces.

A MORNING OF 1649

Charles comes out among his people, looks
Both left and right. Already he has waived
The attendance of an escort. Liberated
From need of lies, he knows this very day

He goes to death, but not to oblivion—
That he is a king. The execution waits;
The morning is both terrible and true.
There is no shiver in his body. He,

Like a good gambler, has always been
Aloof. And he has drunk life to the lees.
Now he moves singly in an armed mob.

The block does not dishonor him. The judges
Are not the Judge. Lightly he nods his head
And smiles. He has done it now so many times.

—A.R.

A UN POETA SAJÓN

La nieve de Nortumbria ha conocido
y ha olvidado la huella de tus pasos
y son innumerables los ocasos
que entre nosotros, gris hermano, han sido.
Lento en la lenta sombra labrarías
metáforas de espadas en los mares
y del horror que mora en los pinares
y de la soledad que traen los días.
¿Dónde buscar tus rasgos y tu nombre?
Ésas son cosas que el antiguo olvido
guarda. Nunca sabré cómo habrá sido
cuando sobre la tierra fuiste un hombre.
Seguiste los caminos del destierro;
ahora sólo eres tu cantar de hierro.

TO A SAXON POET

The snowfalls of Northumbria have known
And have forgotten the imprint of your feet,
And numberless are the suns that now have set
Between your time and mine, my ghostly kinsman.
Slow in the growing shadows you would fashion
Metaphors of swords on the great seas
And of the horror lurking in the pine trees
And of the loneliness the days brought in.
Where can your features and your name be found?
These are things buried in oblivion.
Now I shall never know how it must have been
For you as a living man who walked his ground.
Exiled, you wandered through your lonely ways.
Now you live only in your iron lays.

—A.R.

BUENOS AIRES

Antes, yo te buscaba en tus confines
que lindan con la tarde y la llanura
y en la verja que guarda una frescura
antigua de cedrones y jazmines.
En la memoria de Palermo estabas,
en su mitología de un pasado
de baraja y puñal y en el dorado
bronce de las inútiles aldabas,
con su mano y sortija. Te sentía
en los patios del Sur y en la creciente
sombra que desdibuja lentamente
su larga recta, al declinar el día.
Ahora estás en mí. Eres mi vaga
suerte, esas cosas que la muerte apaga.

BUENOS AIRES

Before, I looked for you within your limits
bounded by the sunset and the plain
and in the fenced yards holding an old-time
coolness of jasmine and of cedar shade.
In the memory of Palermo you were there,
in its mythology of a lost past
of cards and daggers and in the golden
bronze weight of the useless door knockers
with their hands and rings. I felt a sense of you
in the Southside patios and in the lengthening
shadows that ever so slowly obscured
their long right angles as the sun went down.
You are inside me now. You are my blurred
fate, all those things death will obliterate.

—S.K.

BUENOS AIRES

Y la ciudad, ahora, es como un plano
de mis humillaciones y fracasos;
desde esa puerta he visto los ocasos
y ante ese mármol he aguardado en vano.
Aquí el incierto ayer y el hoy distinto
me han deparado los comunes casos
de toda suerte humana; aquí mis pasos
urden su incalculable laberinto.
Aquí la tarde cenicienta espera
el fruto que le debe la mañana;
aquí mi sombra en la no menos vana
sombra final se perderá, ligera.
No nos une el amor sino el espanto;
será por eso que la quiero tanto.

BUENOS AIRES

And now, for me, the city is like a map
of all my failures and humiliations;
from that doorway I watched the sun go down
and next to that statue I waited in vain.
Here unreliable yesterday and different
today have dealt me the same hand they do
to anyone; here is where my steps
weave their incalculable labyrinth.
Here is where the ashen evening awaits
the fruit it has been promised by tomorrow;
here's where my weightless shadow will be lost
in the final shadow, which is no less vain.
It's not love that unites us but our fear;
that must be why I hold this place so dear.

—S.K.

AL HIJO

No soy yo quien te engendra. Son los muertos.
Son mi padre, su padre y sus mayores;
son los que un largo dédalo de amores
trazaron desde Adán y los desiertos
de Caín y de Abel, en una aurora
tan antigua que ya es mitología,
y llegan, sangre y médula, a este día
del porvenir, en que te engendro ahora.
Siento su multitud. Somos nosotros
y, entre nosotros, tú y los venideros
hijos que has de engendrar. Los postrimeros
y los del rojo Adán. Soy esos otros,
también. La eternidad está en las cosas
del tiempo, que son formas presurosas.

TO THE SON

It was not I who begot you. It was the dead—
my father, and his father, and their forebears,
all those who through a labyrinth of loves
descend from Adam and the desert wastes
of Cain and Abel, in a dawn so ancient
it has become mythology by now,
to arrive, blood and marrow, at this day
in the future, in which I now beget you.
I feel their multitudes. They are who we are,
and you among us, you and the sons to come
that you will beget. The latest in the line
and in red Adam's line. I too am those others.
Eternity is present in the things
of time and its impatient happenings.

— A.R.

LOS COMPADRITOS MUERTOS

Siguen apuntalando la recova
del Paseo de Julio, sombras vanas
en eterno altercado con hermanas
sombras o con el hambre, esa otra loba.
Cuando el último sol es amarillo
en la frontera de los arrabales,
vuelven a su crepúsculo, fatales
y muertos, a su puta y su cuchillo.
Perduran en apócrifas historias,
en un modo de andar, en el rasguido
de una cuerda, en un rostro, en un silbido,
en pobres cosas y en oscuras glorias.
En el íntimo patio de la parra
cuando la mano templa la guitarra.

DEAD HOODLUMS

They go on leaning against the market stands
on the Paseo de Julio, those vain shades
in an eternal argument with sister
shades or with that other she-wolf, hunger.
When the last sun is going down yellow
out there at the edges of the slums,
they slip back into their twilight, deadly
and dead, back to their whores and their knives.
They go on living in apocryphal stories
and in a way of walking, in the strumming
of strings, or in a face, or in a whistle,
in obscure glories and the poorest things.
In an intimate, grapevine-shaded patio
when someone's hand is tuning a guitar.

— S.K.

ELOGIO DE LA SOMBRA

IN PRAISE OF DARKNESS

(1969)

NEW ENGLAND, 1967

Han cambiado las formas de mi sueño;
ahora son oblicuas casas rojas
y el delicado bronce de las hojas
y el casto invierno y el piadoso leño.
Como en el día séptimo, la tierra
es buena. En los crepúsculos persiste
algo que casi no es, osado y triste,
un antiguo rumor de Biblia y guerra.
Pronto (nos dicen) llegará la nieve
y América me espera en cada esquina,
pero siento en la tarde que declina
el hoy tan lento y el ayer tan breve.
Buenos Aires, yo sigo caminando
por tus esquinas, sin por qué ni cuándo.

Cambridge, 1967.

NEW ENGLAND, 1967

The forms and colors of my dreams have changed;
now there are red houses side by side
and the fragile bronze of the dying leaves
and the chaste winter and the righteous firewood.
As on the seventh day, the earth is good.
Deep in the twilight something carries on
that nearly does not exist, bold and sad,
an old murmur of Bibles and of war.
Soon (they say) the first snow will arrive;
America waits for me on every street,
but I feel in the falling light of afternoon
today so long and yesterday so brief.
Buenos Aires, it is along your streets
I go on walking, not knowing why or when.

—S.K.

JAMES JOYCE

En un día del hombre están los días
del tiempo, desde aquel inconcebible
día inicial del tiempo, en que un terrible
Dios prefijó los días y agonías
hasta aquel otro en que el ubicuo río
del tiempo terrenal torne a su fuente,
que es lo Eterno, y se apague en el presente,
el futuro, el ayer, lo que ahora es mío.
Entre el alba y la noche está la historia
universal. Desde la noche veo
a mis pies los caminos del hebreo,
Cartago aniquilada, Infierno y Gloria.
Dame, Señor, coraje y alegría
para escalar la cumbre de este día.

Cambridge, 1968.

JAMES JOYCE

In one day of mankind are all the days
of time, from that unimaginable
first day of time, when a formidable
God prearranged the days and agonies,
to that other day when the perpetual river
of earthly time flows round to its headwaters,
the Eternal, and is extinguished in the present,
the future, the past, the passing—what is now mine.
The story of the world is told from dawn
to darkness. From the depths of night I've seen
at my feet the wanderings of the Jews,
Carthage destroyed, Hell, and Heaven's bliss.
Grant me, Lord, the courage and the joy
I need to scale the summit of this day.

—S.K.

RICARDO GÜIRALDES

Nadie podrá olvidar su cortesía;
era la no buscada, la primera
forma de su bondad, la verdadera
cifra de un alma clara como el día.

No he de olvidar tampoco la bizarra
serenidad, el fino rostro fuerte,
las luces de la gloria y de la muerte,
la mano interrogando la guitarra.

Como en el puro sueño de un espejo
(tú eres la realidad, yo su reflejo)
te veo conversando con nosotros

en Quintana. Ahí estás, mágico y muerto.
Tuyo, Ricardo, ahora es el abierto
campo de ayer, el alba de los potros.

RICARDO GÜIRALDES

No one could forget his courtesy;
it was the unsought and the primary
form his goodness took, the truest sign
of a soul as clear as the day is bright.

Nor will I soon forget his gallant air
of serenity, the strength of his fine face,
the shining lights of glory and of death,
his hand interrogating a guitar.

As in the pure dream of a mirror image
(you're the reality, I its reflection)
I see you talking with us on Quintana

Street. There you are, magical and dead.
Yesterday's open countryside is yours,
Ricardo, in the dawn of the wild colts.

—S.K.

LABERINTO

No habrá nunca una puerta. Estás adentro
y el alcázar abarca el universo
y no tiene ni anverso ni reverso
ni externo muro ni secreto centro.
No esperes que el rigor de tu camino
que tercamente se bifurca en otro,
que tercamente se bifurca en otro,
tendrá fin. Es de hierro tu destino
como tu juez. No aguardes la embestida
del toro que es un hombre y cuya extraña
forma plural da horror a la maraña
de interminable piedra entretejida.
No existe. Nada esperes. Ni siquiera
en el negro crepúsculo la fiera.

LABYRINTH

There'll never be a door. You are inside
and the fortress contains the universe
and has no other side nor any back
nor any outer wall nor secret core.
Do not expect the rigor of your path,
which stubbornly splits into another one,
which stubbornly splits into another one,
to have an end. Your fate is ironclad
like your judge. Do not expect the charge
of the bull that is a man and whose strange
plural form fills the thicket of endless
interwoven stone with your own horror.
It does not exist. Expect nothing. Not
even the beast obscured by the black dusk.

— S.K.

LAS COSAS

El bastón, las monedas, el llavero,
la dócil cerradura, las tardías
notas que no leerán los pocos días
que me quedan, los naipes y el tablero,
un libro y en sus páginas la ajada
violeta, monumento de una tarde
sin duda inolvidable y ya olvidada,
el rojo espejo occidental en que arde
una ilusoria aurora. ¡Cuántas cosas,
limas, umbrales, atlas, copas, clavos,
nos sirven como tácitos esclavos,
ciegas y extrañamente sigilosas!
Durarán más allá de nuestro olvido;
no sabrán nunca que nos hemos ido.

THINGS

My cane, my pocket change, this ring of keys,
The obedient lock, the belated notes
The few days left to me will not find time
To read, the deck of cards, the chessboard,
A book and crushed in its pages the withered
Violet, monument to an evening
Undoubtedly unforgettable, now forgotten,
The mirror in the west where a red sunrise
Blazes its illusion. How many things,
Files, doorsills, atlases, wineglasses, nails,
Serve us like slaves who never say a word,
Blind and so mysteriously reserved.
They will endure beyond our vanishing;
And they will never know that we have gone.

        —S.K.

A ISRAEL

¿Quién me dirá si estás en el perdido
laberinto de ríos seculares
de mi sangre, Israel? ¿Quién los lugares
que mi sangre y tu sangre han recorrido?
No importa. Sé que estás en el sagrado
libro que abarca el tiempo y que la historia
del rojo Adán rescata y la memoria
y la agonía del Crucificado.
En ese libro estás, que es el espejo
de cada rostro que sobre él se inclina
y del rostro de Dios, que en su complejo
y arduo cristal, terrible se adivina.
Salve, Israel, que guardas la muralla
de Dios, en la pasión de tu batalla.

TO ISRAEL

Who'll tell me whether you are in the lost
labyrinth of secular rivers in
my blood, Israel? Who can tell me where
my blood and your blood have flowed together?
It doesn't matter. I know you are in the sacred
book that contains time and that rescues
red Adam's story and the memory
and the agony of the Crucified.
You are in that book, which is the mirror
of every face that looks into its pages
and of God's face, who in his intricate
harsh crystal can be terribly divined.
Be safe, Israel, as you guard the wall
of God in all the passion of your fight.

—s.k.

ACEVEDO

Campos de mis abuelos y que guardan
todavía su nombre de Acevedo,
indefinidos campos que no puedo
del todo imaginar. Mis años tardan
y no he mirado aún esas cansadas
leguas de polvo y patria que mis muertos
vieron desde el caballo, esos abiertos
caminos, sus ponientes y alboradas.
La llanura es ubicua. Los he visto
en Iowa, en el Sur, en tierra hebrea,
en aquel saucedal de Galilea
que hollaron los humanos pies de Cristo.
No los perdí. Son míos. Los poseo
en el olvido, en un casual deseo.

ACEVEDO

Lands of my grandfathers that even now
keep as their name the name Acevedo,
vague landscapes I am not completely able
to imagine. My years slowly go by
and I have yet to see those weary miles
of dust and of the homeland my dead ones
saw from their horses, those open roads,
their darkening sundowns and rising dawns.
The plains are everywhere. I have seen them
in Iowa, in the South, in the Hebrew lands,
and in that willow grove in Galilee
whose ground the human feet of Christ once trod.
I never lost them. They are mine. I have them
in oblivion, in an accidental wish.

—S.K.

RITTER, TOD UND TEUFEL

Bajo el yelmo quimérico el severo
perfil es cruel como la cruel espada
que aguarda. Por la selva despojada
cabalga imperturbable el caballero.

Torpe y furtiva, la caterva obscena
lo ha cercado: el Demonio de serviles
ojos, los laberínticos reptiles
y el blanco anciano del reloj de arena.

Caballero de hierro, quien te mira
sabe que en ti no mora la mentira
ni el pálido temor. Tu dura suerte

es mandar y ultrajar. Eres valiente
y no serás indigno ciertamente,
alemán, del Demonio y de la Muerte.

"KNIGHT, DEATH, AND THE DEVIL"

Under the unreal helmet the severe
Profile is cruel like the cruel sword
Waiting, poised. Through the stripped forest
Rides the horseman unperturbed.

Clumsily, furtively, the obscene mob
Closes in on him: the Devil with servile
Eyes, the labyrinthine reptiles
And the ashen old man with the hourglass.

Iron rider, whoever looks at you
Knows that in you neither the lie
Nor pale fear dwells. Your hard fate

Is to command and offend. You are brave
And you are certainly not unworthy,
German, of the Devil and of Death.

— S.K.

EL ORO DE LOS TIGRES

THE GOLD OF THE TIGERS

(1972)

A JOHN KEATS
(1795–1821)

Desde el principio hasta la joven muerte
la terrible belleza te acechaba
como a los otros la propicia suerte
o la adversa. En las albas te esperaba
de Londres, en las páginas casuales
de un diccionario de mitología,
en las comunes dádivas del día,
en un rostro, una voz, y en los mortales
labios de Fanny Brawne. Oh sucesivo
y arrebatado Keats, que el tiempo ciega,
el alto ruiseñor y la urna griega
serán tu eternidad, oh fugitivo.
Fuiste el fuego. En la pánica memoria
no eres hoy la ceniza. Eres la gloria.

TO JOHN KEATS
(1795–1821)

From the beginning to your early death
a terrible beauty lay in wait for you
as good or bad luck lay in wait for others.
That beauty waited for you in the dawns
of London, or by chance in the pages of
a dictionary of mythology,
in the ordinary gifts of a normal day,
or in a face, a voice, the mortal lips
of Fanny Brawne. O posthumous Keats
snatched away from earth, blinded by time,
the nightingale on high and the Greek urn
are your eternity, o fleeting one.
You were the fire. In Panic memory
you are not ashes now. You are glory.

—S.K.

ON HIS BLINDNESS

Indigno de los astros y del ave
que surca el hondo azul, ahora secreto,
de esas líneas que son el alfabeto
que ordenan otros y del mármol grave
cuyo dintel mis ya gastados ojos
pierden en su penumbra, de las rosas
invisibles y de las silenciosas
multitudes de oros y de rojos
soy, pero no de las Mil Noches y Una
que abren mares y auroras en mi sombra
ni de Walt Whitman, ese Adán que nombra
las criaturas que son bajo la luna,
ni de los blancos dones del olvido
ni del amor que espero y que no pido.

ON HIS BLINDNESS

Unworthy of the stars and of the bird
cutting a path through blue sky, now concealed,
and of those lines that are the alphabet
ordered by others, and of the grave marble
whose threshold my now exhausted eyesight
misses in its penumbra, of the invisible
roses and of the silent multitudes
of golds and reds, it's true, I am unworthy,
but not of the One Thousand and One Nights
that open dawns and oceans in my darkness
nor of Walt Whitman, that Adam whose task
is to name all the creatures under the moon,
nor of the white gifts of oblivion
nor love, for which I hope but do not ask.

—s.k.

LO PERDIDO

¿Dónde estará mi vida, la que pudo
haber sido y no fue, la venturosa
o la de triste horror, esa otra cosa
que pudo ser la espada o el escudo
y que no fue? ¿Dónde estará el perdido
antepasado persa o el noruego,
dónde el azar de no quedarme ciego,
dónde el ancla y el mar, dónde el olvido
de ser quien soy? ¿Dónde estará la pura
noche que al rudo labrador confía
el iletrado y laborioso día,
según lo quiere la literatura?
Pienso también en esa compañera
que me esperaba, y que tal vez me espera.

WHAT IS LOST

I wonder where my life is, the one that could
have been and never was, the daring one
or the one of gloomy dread, that other thing
which could as well have been the sword or shield
but never was? I wonder where is my lost
Persian or Norwegian ancestor,
where is the chance of my not being blind,
where is the anchor, the ocean, where the forgetting
to be who I am? I wonder where the pure
night is that the unlettered working day
entrusts to the rough laborer so that he
can also feel the love of literature.
I also think about a certain mate
who waited for me once, perhaps still waits.

—S.K.

J. M.

En cierta calle hay cierta firme puerta
con su timbre y su número preciso
y un sabor a perdido Paraíso,
que en los atardeceres no está abierta
a mi paso. Cumplida la jornada,
una esperada voz me esperaría
en la disgregación de cada día
y en la paz de la noche enamorada.
Esas cosas no son. Otra es mi suerte:
las vagas horas, la memoria impura,
el abuso de la literatura
y en el confín la no gustada muerte.
Sólo esa piedra quiero. Sólo pido
las dos abstractas fechas y el olvido.

J. M.

On a certain street there is a certain door
shut with its bell and its exact address
and with a flavor of lost Paradise,
which in the early evening I can never
open to enter. The day's work at its end,
a voice I waited for would wait for me
there in the dissolution of every day
and in the stillness of the beloved night.
Those things are no more. This is my fate:
the blurry hours, impure memories,
habitual abuse of literature
and at the edge my yet to be tasted death.
That stone is all I want. All I request
are the two abstract dates and nothingness.

—S.K.

RELIGIO MEDICI, 1643

Defiéndeme Señor. (El vocativo
no implica a Nadie. Es sólo una palabra
de este ejercicio que el desgano labra
y que en la tarde del temor escribo.)
Defiéndeme de mí. Ya lo dijeron
Montaigne y Browne y un español que ignoro;
algo me queda aún de todo ese oro
que mis ojos de sombra recogieron.
Defiéndeme, Señor, del impaciente
apetito de ser mármol y olvido;
defiéndeme de ser el que ya he sido,
el que ya he sido irreparablemente.
No de la espada o de la roja lanza
defiéndeme, sino de la esperanza.

RELIGIO MEDICI, 1643

Save me, O Lord. (That I use a name for you
does not imply a Being. It's just a word
from that vocabulary the tenuous use,
and that I use now, in an evening of panic.)
Save me from myself. Others have asked the same—
Montaigne, Sir Thomas Browne, an unknown Spaniard.
Something remains in me of these golden visions
that my fading eyesight can still recognize.
Save me, O Lord, from that impatient urge:
to yield myself to tombstones and oblivion.
Save me from facing all that I have been,
that person I have been irreparably.
Not from the sword-thrust or the bloodstained lance.
Save me, at least, from all those golden fictions.

—A.R.

AL TRISTE

Ahí está lo que fue: la terca espada
del sajón y su métrica de hierro,
los mares y las islas del destierro
del hijo de Laertes, la dorada

luna del persa y los sin fin jardines
de la filosofía y de la historia,
el oro sepulcral de la memoria
y en la sombra el olor de los jazmines.

Y nada de eso importa. El resignado
ejercicio del verso no te salva
ni las aguas del sueño ni la estrella

que en la arrasada noche olvida el alba.
Una sola mujer es tu cuidado,
igual a las demás, pero que es ella.

TO THE SAD MAN

There is what was: the rigid sword
of the Saxon and his ironclad measure,
the oceans and Laertes' son in exile
on his various islands, the golden

moon of Persia and the boundless gardens
of philosophy and of history,
the sepulchral gold of memory
and in the shadows the scent of jasmine.

And none of that matters. The resigned
practice of poetry will not save you
nor the waters of sleep nor the star

in the satiny night that dawn forgets.
All you care about is just one woman,
the same as all the others, only her.

—S.K.

EL MAR

El mar. El joven mar. El mar de Ulises
y el de aquel otro Ulises que la gente
del Islam apodó famosamente
Es-Sindibad del Mar. El mar de grises
olas de Erico el Rojo, alto en su proa,
y el de aquel caballero que escribía
a la vez la epopeya y la elegía
de su patria, en la ciénaga de Goa.
El mar de Trafalgar. El que Inglaterra
cantó a lo largo de su larga historia,
el arduo mar que ensangrentó de gloria
en el diario ejercicio de la guerra.
El incesante mar que en la serena
mañana surca la infinita arena.

THE SEA

The sea. The young sea. The sea of Ulysses
and of that other Ulysses whom the people
of Islam famously gave the name
Sinbad the Sailor. The gray-waved sea
of Eric the Red, high in his ship's prow,
and the sea of that gentleman who wrote
at once the epic and the elegy
for his country, in the bog of Goa.
The sea of Trafalgar. The sea that England
sang for the length of its long history,
the strenuous sea turned bloody with glory
in the everyday exercise of war.
The incessant sea that in the serene
morning plows the sands that never end.

—S.K.

A UN GATO

No son más silenciosos los espejos
ni más furtiva el alba aventurera;
eres, bajo la luna, esa pantera
que nos es dado divisar de lejos.
Por obra indescifrable de un decreto
divino, te buscamos vanamente;
más remoto que el Ganges y el poniente,
tuya es la soledad, tuyo el secreto.
Tu lomo condesciende a la morosa
caricia de mi mano. Has admitido,
desde esa eternidad que ya es olvido,
el amor de la mano recelosa.
En otro tiempo estás. Eres el dueño
de un ámbito cerrado como un sueño.

TO A CAT

Mirrors are not more wrapt in silences
nor the arriving dawn more secretive;
you, in the moonlight, are that panther figure
which we can only spy at from a distance.
By the mysterious functioning of some
divine decree, we seek you out in vain;
remoter than the Ganges or the sunset,
yours is the solitude, yours is the secret.
Your back allows the tentative caress
my hand extends. And you have condescended,
since that eternity, by now forgotten,
to take love from a flattering human hand.
You live in other time, lord of your realm—
a world as closed and separate as dream.

—A.R.

AL COYOTE

Durante siglos la infinita arena
de los muchos desiertos ha sufrido
tus pasos numerosos y tu aullido
de gris chacal o de insaciada hiena.
¿Durante siglos? Miento. Esa furtiva
substancia, el tiempo, no te alcanza, lobo;
tuyo es el puro ser, tuyo el arrobo,
nuestra, la torpe vida sucesiva.
Fuiste un ladrido casi imaginario
en el confín de arena de Arizona
donde todo es confín, donde se encona
tu perdido ladrido solitario.
Símbolo de una noche que fue mía,
sea tu vago espejo esta elegía.

TO COYOTE

Down through the centuries the infinite sands
of so many deserts have endured the tracks
of your countless steps and your primal howl
of a ravenous hyena or gray jackal.
Through centuries? I'm lying. That furtive
substance, time, can't touch you, wolf;
yours is the state of pure enchanted being,
ours, the dull, slow life that trudges on.
You were an almost imaginary barking
at the far edge of the Arizona sand
where everything is edge, where anger rankles
and inflames your lost, solitary cry.
Symbol of a night I once spent there,
let this elegy be your cloudy mirror.

— S.K.

LA ROSA PROFUNDA

THE UNENDING ROSE

(1975)

YO

La calavera, el corazón secreto,
los caminos de sangre que no veo,
los túneles del sueño, ese Proteo,
las vísceras, la nuca, el esqueleto.
Soy esas cosas. Increíblemente
soy también la memoria de una espada
y la de un solitario sol poniente
que se dispersa en oro, en sombra, en nada.
Soy el que ve las proas desde el puerto;
soy los contados libros, los contados
grabados por el tiempo fatigados;
soy el que envidia a los que ya se han muerto.
Más raro es ser el hombre que entrelaza
palabras en un cuarto de una casa.

I

The skull within, the secret, shuttered heart,
the byways of the blood I never see,
the underworld of dreaming, that Proteus,
the nape, the viscera, the skeleton.
I am all those things. Amazingly,
I am too the memory of a sword
and of a solitary, falling sun,
turning itself to gold, then gray, then nothing.
I am the one who sees the approaching ships
from harbor. And I am the dwindled books,
the rare engravings worn away by time;
the one who envies those already dead.
Stranger to be the man who interlaces
such words as these, in some room in a house.

—A.R.

COSMOGONÍA

Ni tiniebla ni caos. La tiniebla
requiere ojos que ven, como el sonido
y el silencio requieren el oído,
y el espejo, la forma que lo puebla.
Ni el espacio ni el tiempo. Ni siquiera
una divinidad que premedita
el silencio anterior a la primera
noche del tiempo, que será infinita.
El gran río de Heráclito el Oscuro
su irrevocable curso no ha emprendido,
que del pasado fluye hacia el futuro,
que del olvido fluye hacia el olvido.
Algo que ya padece. Algo que implora.
Después la historia universal. Ahora.

COSMOGONY

No darkness and no chaos. Darkness demands
eyes that can see, the same way sound and silence
demand ears with the power of hearing and
the mirror a form to fill it with an image.
No space, no time. Not even a divine
inventor of the original silence
preceding the first night of beginning
time, a night that must be infinite.
The great river of Heraclitus the Obscure
has not set out on its relentless course,
flowing from the past toward the future,
flowing from oblivion toward oblivion.
Something suffering. Something that implores.
And then the history of the universe. Now.

—S.K.

LA PANTERA

Tras los fuertes barrotes la pantera
repetirá el monótono camino
que es (pero no lo sabe) su destino
de negra joya, aciaga y prisionera.
Son miles las que pasan y son miles
las que vuelven, pero es una y eterna
la pantera fatal que en su caverna
traza la recta que un eterno Aquiles
traza en el sueño que ha soñado el griego.
No sabe que hay praderas y montañas
de ciervos cuyas trémulas entrañas
deleitarían su apetito ciego.
En vano es vario el orbe. La jornada
que cumple cada cual ya fue fijada.

THE PANTHER

Behind the strong bars of her cage the panther
will go on pacing, pacing back and forth,
which is (without her knowing it) her destiny
of a black jewel fated to be a prisoner.
Thousands of panthers are pacing this way
and that, but the one panther in her den
is singular and eternal as she traces
the straight line traced by an eternal
Achilles in the dream dreamed by the Greek.
She doesn't know there are plains and mountains
alive with deer whose trembling bellies would
delight her blindly ravenous appetite.
The world's variety is vanity.
Everyone's daily round is long since set.

—S.K.

EL BISONTE

Montañoso, abrumado, indescifrable,
rojo como la brasa que se apaga,
anda fornido y lento por la vaga
soledad de su páramo incansable.
El armado testuz levanta. En este
antiguo toro de durmiente ira,
veo a los hombres rojos del Oeste
y a los perdidos hombres de Altamira.
Luego pienso que ignora el tiempo humano,
cuyo espejo espectral es la memoria.
El tiempo no lo toca ni la historia
de su decurso, tan variable y vano.
Intemporal, innumerable, cero,
es el postrer bisonte y el primero.

THE BISON

Powerful, unknowable, mountainous,
red as a bed of coals whose fire fades,
it roams, huge and slow, over the vague
solitude of its tireless wilderness.
It raises its armed head. Inside this
ancient bull built out of dormant rage,
I can discern the red men of the West
and the lost men of the Altamira caves.
Then I think it can't know human time,
whose spectral mirror is our memory.
Time never touches it nor the history
of its wanderings, so aimless and so cursed
with uselessness. Timeless, numberless, zero,
it is the final bison, and the first.

— S.K.

ESPADAS

Gram, Durendal, Joyeuse, Excalibur.
Sus viejas guerras andan por el verso,
que es la única memoria. El universo
las siembra por el Norte y por el Sur.
En la espada persiste la porfía
de la diestra viril, hoy polvo y nada;
en el hierro o el bronce, la estocada
que fue sangre de Adán un primer día.
Gestas he enumerado de lejanas
espadas cuyos hombres dieron muerte
a reyes y a serpientes. Otra suerte
de espadas hay, murales y cercanas.
Déjame, espada, usar contigo el arte;
yo, que no he merecido manejarte.

SWORDS

Gram, Durendal, Joyeuse, Excalibur.
Their ancient wars live on in poetry,
which is the only memory. The world
scatters their seeds over the North and South.
In the sword the swordsman's strong right hand persists
even though now he is nothing but dust;
in iron or in bronze there is a thrust
that drew the blood of Adam one first day.
I have recounted exploits of faraway
swords whose men delivered death to kings,
serpents and snakes. There is another fate
for swords, to be in murals and on walls.
Permit me, sword, to use you in my art;
I, who to wield you haven't earned the right.

—S.K.

SOY

Soy el que sabe que no es menos vano
que el vano observador que en el espejo
de silencio y cristal sigue el reflejo
o el cuerpo (da lo mismo) del hermano.
Soy, tácitos amigos, el que sabe
que no hay otra venganza que el olvido
ni otro perdón. Un dios ha concedido
al odio humano esta curiosa llave.
Soy el que pese a tan ilustres modos
de errar, no ha descifrado el laberinto
singular y plural, arduo y distinto,
del tiempo, que es de uno y es de todos.
Soy el que es nadie, el que no fue una espada
en la guerra. Soy eco, olvido, nada.

I AM

I am he who knows himself no less vain
than the vain looker-on who in the mirror
of glass and silence follows the reflection
or body (it's the same thing) of his brother.
I am, my silent friends, the one who knows
there is no other pardon or revenge
than sheer oblivion. A god has granted
this odd solution to all human hates.
Despite my many wondrous wanderings,
I am the one who never has unraveled
the labyrinth of time, singular, plural,
grueling, strange, one's own and everyone's.
I am no one. I did not wield a sword
in battle. I am echo, emptiness, nothing.

—A.R.

SUEÑA ALONSO QUIJANO

El hombre se despierta de un incierto
sueño de alfanjes y de campo llano
y se toca la barba con la mano
y se pregunta si está herido o muerto.
¿No lo perseguirán los hechiceros
que han jurado su mal bajo la luna?
Nada. Apenas el frío. Apenas una
dolencia de sus años postrimeros.
El hidalgo fue un sueño de Cervantes
y don Quijote un sueño del hidalgo.
El doble sueño los confunde y algo
está pasando que pasó mucho antes.
Quijano duerme y sueña. Una batalla:
los mares de Lepanto y la metralla.

ALONSO QUIJANO DREAMS

The man wakes up from a confusing dream
of scimitars and a landscape strangely flat
and touches his beard with his one good hand
and wonders if he's been wounded, or been killed.
Is he not being tormented by sorcerers
who've sworn to do him evil under the moon?
Nothing. Scarcely a chill. Scarcely an ache
in the aging bones of his twilight years.
The country squire was a dream dreamed by Cervantes
and Don Quixote a dream of the country squire.
The double dream confuses them and something
is happening that happened long before.
Quijano sleeps and dreams. He is at war:
the seas of Lepanto and the cannon fire.

—S.K.

A UN CÉSAR

En la noche propicia a los lemures
y a las larvas que hostigan a los muertos,
han cuartelado en vano los abiertos
ámbitos de los astros tus augures.
Del toro yugulado en la penumbra
las vísceras en vano han indagado;
en vano el sol de esta mañana alumbra
la espada fiel del pretoriano armado.
En el palacio tu garganta espera
temblorosa el puñal. Ya los confines
del imperio que rigen tus clarines
presienten las plegarias y la hoguera.
De tus montañas el horror sagrado
el tigre de oro y sombra ha profanado.

TO A CAESAR

In the night that is host to evil spirits
and to the larvae that plague the dead,
the open ambits of the stars have given
shelter to their auguries in vain.
The bull slit open in the dimming light
in vain has had its entrails scrutinized;
in vain the morning sunlight flashes on
the faithful sword of the praetorian guard.
Inside the palace your trembling throat awaits
the dagger. Now the finite boundaries
of empire that your clarions claim to govern
can sense their supplications and their pyres.
Out of your mountains the holy terror
has come to curse the gold and shadowed tiger.

—s.k.

PROTEO

Antes que los remeros de Odiseo
fatigaran el mar color de vino
las inasibles formas adivino
de aquel dios cuyo nombre fue Proteo.
Pastor de los rebaños de los mares
y poseedor del don de profecía,
prefería ocultar lo que sabía
y entretejer oráculos dispares.
Urgido por las gentes asumía
la forma de un león o de una hoguera
o de árbol que da sombra a la ribera
o de agua que en el agua se perdía.
De Proteo el egipcio no te asombres,
tú, que eres uno y eres muchos hombres.

PROTEUS

Before the oarsmen of Odysseus
have finished wearing out the wine-dark sea
I have a vision of the slippery forms
of that ungraspable god called Proteus.
Shepherd of the flocks that roam the ocean,
possessor of the gift of prophecy,
he preferred to conceal all that he knew
and weave an array of different oracles.
Pressed by so many people, he assumed
the form of a lion or a bonfire
or a tree shading a riverbank
or water getting lost in other water.
Do not be astonished at Proteus the Egyptian,
you, who are also one and many men.

—S.K.

OTRA VERSIÓN DE PROTEO

Habitador de arenas recelosas,
mitad dios y mitad bestia marina,
ignoró la memoria, que se inclina
sobre el ayer y las perdidas cosas.
Otro tormento padeció Proteo
no menos cruel, saber lo que ya encierra
el porvenir: la puerta que se cierra
para siempre, el troyano y el aqueo.
Atrapado, asumía la inasible
forma del huracán o de la hoguera
o del tigre de oro o la pantera
o de agua que en el agua es invisible.
Tú también estás hecho de inconstantes
ayeres y mañanas. Mientras, antes . . .

ANOTHER VERSION OF PROTEUS

Inhabitant of suspicious, fearful sands,
one half god and the other half sea monster,
his memory eludes him and is leaning
toward the past and over what's been lost.
Proteus suffered yet another torment
no less cruel, to know now what the future
holds: the door that is swinging closed
forever, the Trojan and the Achaean.
Trapped, he took on the ungraspable
form of the hurricane or the bonfire
or the golden tiger or the panther
or water invisibly hidden in other water.
You too are made of ever shifting shapes
of yesterdays and tomorrows. While, before . . .

—S.K.

HABLA UN BUSTO DE JANO

Nadie abriere o cerrare alguna puerta
sin honrar la memoria del Bifronte,
que las preside. Abarco el horizonte
de inciertos mares y de tierra cierta.
Mis dos caras divisan el pasado
y el porvenir. Los veo y son iguales
los hierros, las discordias y los males
que Alguien pudo borrar y no ha borrado
ni borrará. Me faltan las dos manos
y soy de piedra inmóvil. No podría
precisar si contemplo una porfía
futura o la de ayeres hoy lejanos.
Veo mi ruina: la columna trunca
y las caras, que no se verán nunca.

A BUST OF JANUS SPEAKS

No one is to open or close a single door
without homage to me, who see two ways,
doors' tutelary. Horizon lines
of stable land, unstable seas, yield to my gaze.
My two faces penetrate the past,
discern the future. Common to both I see,
drawn swords, evil, discord;
one who could have removed them let them be
and does so still. Missing are my two hands.
I am of stone fixed in place. I cannot say
for sure whether the things that I behold
are future disputes or quarrels of yesterday.
I look about my ruins: truncated column,
faces powerless to glance each other's way.

—A.S.T.

DE QUE NADA SE SABE

La luna ignora que es tranquila y clara
y ni siquiera sabe que es la luna;
la arena, que es la arena. No habrá una
cosa que sepa que su forma es rara.
Las piezas de marfil son tan ajenas
al abstracto ajedrez como la mano
que las rige. Quizá el destino humano
de breves dichas y de largas penas
es instrumento de Otro. Lo ignoramos;
darle nombre de Dios no nos ayuda.
Vanos también son el temor, la duda
y la trunca plegaria que iniciamos.
¿Qué arco habrá arrojado esta saeta
que soy? ¿Qué cumbre puede ser la meta?

OF WHICH NOTHING IS KNOWN

The moon does not know it is calm and bright
and does not even know it is the moon;
the sand, that it is sand. There must not be
a single thing that knows its form is strange.
Ivory chess pieces are as alien from
their abstract game as is the human hand
that moves them. Could it be man's destiny
of brief joys and long sorrows is some Other's
instrument? We don't and cannot know;
calling it God is of no use to us.
Even our fear is in vain, and our doubt
and the prayers we begin but never finish.
What bow released this arrow that I am?
What summit of what mountain is my end?

—S.K.

EL CIEGO

I

Lo han despojado del diverso mundo,
de los rostros, que son lo que eran antes.
De las cercanas calles, hoy distantes,
y del cóncavo azul, ayer profundo.
De los libros le queda lo que deja
la memoria, esa forma del olvido
que retiene el formato, no el sentido,
y que los meros títulos refleja.
El desnivel acecha. Cada paso
puede ser la caída. Soy el lento
prisionero de un tiempo soñoliento
que no marca su aurora ni su ocaso.
Es de noche. No hay otros. Con el verso
debo labrar mi insípido universo.

THE BLIND MAN

I

He is divested of the diverse world,
of faces, which still stay as once they were,
of the adjoining streets, now far away,
and of the concave sky, once infinite.
Of books, he keeps no more than what is left him
by memory, that brother of forgetting,
which keeps the formula but not the feeling,
and which reflects no more than tag and name.
Traps lie in wait for me. My every step
might be a fall. I am a prisoner
shuffling through a time that feels like dream,
taking no note of mornings or of sunsets.
It is night. I am alone. In verse like this,
I must create my insipid universe.

II

Desde mi nacimiento, que fue el noventa y nueve
de la cóncavas parras y el aljibe profundo,
el tiempo minucioso, que en la memoria es breve,
me fue hurtando las formas visibles de este mundo.
Los días y las noches limaron los perfiles
de las letras humanas y los rostros amados;
en vano interrogaron mis ojos agotados
las vanas bibliotecas y los vanos atriles.
El azul y el bermejo son ahora una niebla
y dos voces inútiles. El espejo que miro
es una cosa gris. En el jardín aspiro,
amigos, una lóbrega rosa de la tiniebla.
Ahora sólo perduran las formas amarillas
y sólo puedo ver para ver pesadillas.

II

Since I was born, in 1899,
beside the concave vine and the deep cistern,
frittering time, so brief in memory,
kept taking from me all my eye-shaped world.
Both days and nights would wear away the profiles
of human letters and of well-loved faces.
My wasted eyes would ask their useless questions
of pointless libraries and lecterns.
Blue and vermilion both are now a fog,
both useless sounds. The mirror I look into
is gray. I breathe a rose across the garden,
a wistful rose, my friends, out of the twilight.
Only shades of yellow stay with me
and I can see only to look on nightmares.

—A.R.

UN CIEGO

No sé cuál es la cara que me mira
cuando miro la cara del espejo;
no sé qué anciano acecha en su reflejo
con silenciosa y ya cansada ira.
Lento en mi sombra, con la mano exploro
mis invisibles rasgos. Un destello
me alcanza. He vislumbrado tu cabello
que es de ceniza o es aún de oro.
Repito que he perdido solamente
la vana superficie de las cosas.
El consuelo es de Milton y es valiente,
pero pienso en las letras y en las rosas.
Pienso que si pudiera ver mi cara
sabría quién soy en esta tarde rara.

A BLIND MAN

I do not know what face is looking back
whenever I look at the face in the mirror;
I do not know what old face seeks its image
in silent and already weary anger.
Slow in my blindness, with my hand I feel
the contours of my face. A flash of light
gets through to me. I have made out your hair,
color of ash and at the same time, gold.
I say again that I have lost no more
than the inconsequential skin of things.
These wise words come from Milton, and are noble,
but then I think of letters and of roses.
I think, too, that if I could see my features,
I would know who I am, this precious afternoon.

— A.R.

ALL OUR YESTERDAYS

Quiero saber de quién es mi pasado.
¿De cuál de los que fui? ¿Del ginebrino
que trazó algún hexámetro latino
que los lustrales años han borrado?
¿Es de aquel niño que buscó en la entera
biblioteca del padre las puntuales
curvaturas del mapa y las ferales
formas que son el tigre y la pantera?
¿O de aquel otro que empujó una puerta
detrás de la que un hombre se moría
para siempre, y besó en el blanco día
la cara que se va y la cara muerta?
Soy los que ya no son. Inútilmente
soy en la tarde esa perdida gente.

ALL OUR YESTERDAYS

I want to know whose past belongs to me.
Which one of those was I? The Genevan
who wrote out some hexameter in Latin
that the purifying years have rubbed away?
Was I that boy who searched through his father's
entire library for the precise lines
and contours of the map and for the wild
forms that are the tiger and the panther?
Or was I the one who opened a door
behind which a man lay perishing
forever, and kissed in the white light of day
the dying face and the face that had gone away?
I am the ones that now are not. This evening,
uselessly, I am all of those lost beings.

—S.K.

EN MEMORIA DE ANGÉLICA

¡Cuántas posibles vidas se habrán ido
en esta pobre y diminuta muerte,
cuántas posibles vidas que la suerte
daría a la memoria o al olvido!
Cuando yo muera morirá un pasado;
con esta flor un porvenir ha muerto
en las aguas que ignoran, un abierto
porvenir por los astros arrasado.
Yo, como ella, muero de infinitos
destinos que el azar no me depara;
busca mi sombra los gastados mitos
de una patria que siempre dio la cara.
Un breve mármol cuida su memoria;
sobre nosotros crece, atroz, la historia.

IN MEMORY OF ANGÉLICA

I wonder how many possible lives have gone
out of the world with this poor little death,
how many possible lives that luck or fate
would give to memory or oblivion!
When I die only a past will disappear;
with this flower a future has expired
in waters that know nothing, an opening
future laid waste by the indifferent stars.
Like her, I am dying from an infinite
number of destinies I've missed by chance;
my shade is seeking the exhausted myths
of a country that always did what it must.
A marble slab cares for her memory;
over us grows, hideously, history.

—S.K.

AL ESPEJO

¿Por qué persistes, incesante espejo?
¿Por qué duplicas, misterioso hermano,
el menor movimiento de mi mano?
¿Por qué en la sombra el súbito reflejo?
Eres el otro yo de que habla el griego
y acechas desde siempre. En la tersura
del agua incierta o del cristal que dura
me buscas y es inútil estar ciego.
El hecho de no verte y de saberte
te agrega horror, cosa de magia que osas
multiplicar la cifra de las cosas
que somos y que abarcan nuestra suerte.
Cuando esté muerto, copiarás a otro.
y luego a otro, a otro, a otro, a otro . . .

TO A MIRROR

Why do you go on, neverending mirror?
Why do you duplicate, mysterious brother,
the slightest movement of my moving hand?
Why do you flash reflections in the dark?
You are the other I the Greek spoke of
and you've been spying on me since forever.
With your smooth, fluid water or solid glass
you seek me out and being blind is useless.
Not seeing you yet knowing you are there
is horrible, you ghostly thing that dares
to multiply the sum of everything
we are and which will add up to our fate.
When I am dead you will reflect another,
then another, and another, and another . . .

— S . K .

EL TESTIGO

Desde su sueño el hombre ve al gigante
de un sueño que soñado fue en Bretaña
y apresta el corazón para la hazaña
y le clava la espuela a Rocinante.

El viento hace girar las laboriosas
aspas que el hombre gris ha acometido.
Rueda el rocín; la lanza se ha partido
y es una cosa más entre las cosas.

Yace en la tierra el hombre de armadura;
lo ve caer el hijo de un vecino,
que no sabrá el final de la aventura

y que a las Indias llevará el destino.
Perdido en el confín de otra llanura
se dirá que fue un sueño el del molino.

THE WITNESS

From inside his dream the man can see the giant
In a dream that was first dreamed in Brittany
And he prepares his heart for the great deed
And digs his spurs deep into Rocinante.

The wind turns round the heavy, laboring
Arms that the gray rider has assaulted.
The horse somersaults down; the lance is broken
And becomes one more thing among other things.

The man in armor sprawls breathless on the ground;
The son of a farmer watches as he falls,
But will not know how the adventure ends.

Destiny will carry him to the Indies.
Lost in the confines of another plain
He will call that man and windmill a mere dream.

—E.G.

EFIALTES

En el fondo del sueño están los sueños. Cada
noche quiero perderme en las aguas obscuras
que me lavan del día, pero bajo esas puras
aguas que nos conceden la penúltima Nada
late en la hora gris la obscena maravilla.
Puede ser un espejo con mi rostro distinto,
puede ser la creciente cárcel de un laberinto,
puede ser un jardín. Siempre es la pesadilla.
Su horror no es de este mundo. Algo que no se
nombra me alcanza desde ayeres de mito y de neblina;
la imagen detestada perdura en la retina
e infama la vigilia como infamó la sombra.
¿Por qué brota de mí cuando el cuerpo reposa
y el alma queda sola, esta insensata rosa?

INCUBUS

The dreams dwell in the lower depths of sleep. Every
night I try to lose myself in the dark waters
that wash the day from me, but beneath those pure
waters that grant us the gift of near Nothingness
the obscene wonder throbs in the gray hours.
It can be a mirror with my face, but different,
it can be the spreading prison of a labyrinth,
it can be a garden. It is a nightmare always.
Its horror is not of this world. Something nameless
comes over me from yesterdays of myth and mist;
the despicable image lingers on my retina
and slanders consciousness as it slandered the dark.
Why, when my body finally finds repose,
does my soul, alone, bring forth this senseless rose?

—S.K.

LA CIERVA BLANCA

¿De qué agreste balada de la verde Inglaterra,
de qué lámina persa, de qué región arcana
de las noches y días que nuestro ayer encierra,
vino la cierva blanca, que soñé esta mañana?
Duraría un segundo. La vi cruzar el prado
y perderse en el oro de una tarde ilusoria,
leve criatura hecha de un poco de memoria
y de un poco de olvido, cierva de un solo lado.
Los númenes que rigen este curioso mundo
me dejaron soñarte pero no ser tu dueño;
tal vez en un recodo del porvenir profundo
te encontraré de nuevo, cierva blanca de un sueño.
Yo también soy un sueño fugitivo que dura
unos días más que el sueño del prado y la blancura.

THE WHITE DEER

From what folk ballad out of green England,
from what Persian print, from what arcane region
of nights and days enclosed in yesterday,
did the white deer come, the one I dreamed this morning?
It lasted but a second. I saw it cross a field
and vanish into the gold of an illusory evening,
a light-footed creature made partly of memory
and partly of forgetting, a deer with just one side.
The mysterious forces that rule this curious world
allowed me to dream you but not to be your master;
perhaps at some bend in the distant future
I'll meet you again, white deer of a dream.
I too am a fleeting dream which scarcely lasts
longer than that of a field and a white flash.

—S.K.

LA MONEDA DE HIERRO

THE IRON COIN

(1976)

CORONEL SUÁREZ

Alta en el alba se alza la severa
faz de metal y de melancolía.
Un perro se desliza por la acera.
Ya no es de noche y no es aún de día.

Suárez mira su pueblo y la llanura
ulterior, las estancias, los potreros,
los rumbos que fatigan los reseros,
el paciente planeta que perdura.

Detrás del simulacro te adivino.
oh joven capitán que fuiste el dueño
de esa batalla que torció el destino:

Junín, resplandeciente como un sueño.
En un confín del vasto Sur persiste
esa alta cosa, vagamente triste.

COLONEL SUÁREZ

High in a dim-lit dawn the dour, harsh face
Looms, composed of melancholy and metal.
A lone dog sidles down the empty sidewalk.
It is no longer night and not yet day.

Suárez contemplates his city and the plain
That lies beyond, the ranches, the horse farms,
The trails that exhaust the weary cattlemen,
The world, the patient planet that endures.

Beyond this appearance I imagine you,
Oh youthful captain, the master in command
Of the battle that turned destiny around:

Junín, as resplendent as a dream.
In a corner of the vast South there persists
That noble thing, a high thing, vaguely sad.

—E.G.

LA PESADILLA

Sueño con un antiguo rey. De hierro
es la corona y muerta la mirada.
Ya no hay caras así. La firme espada
lo acatará, leal como su perro.
No sé si es de Nortumbria o de Noruega.
Sé que es del Norte. La cerrada y roja
barba le cubre el pecho. No me arroja
una mirada su mirada ciega.
¿De qué apagado espejo, de qué nave
de los mares que fueron su aventura,
habrá surgido el hombre gris y grave
que me impone su antaño y su amargura?
Sé que me sueña y que me juzga, erguido.
El día entra en la noche. No se ha ido.

NIGHTMARE

I'm dreaming of an ancient king. His crown
Is iron and his gaze is dead. There are
No faces like that now. And never far
His firm sword guards him, loyal like his hound.
I do not know if he is from Norway
Or Northumberland. But from the north, I know.
His tight red beard covers his chest. And no,
His blind gaze doesn't hurl a gaze my way.
From what extinguished mirror, from what ship
On seas that were his gambling wilderness
Could this man, gray and grave, venture a trip
Forcing on me his past and bitterness?
I know he dreams and judges me, is drawn
Erect. Day breaks up night. He hasn't gone.

—W.B.

LA VÍSPERA

Millares de partículas de arena,
ríos que ignoran el reposo, nieve
más delicada que una sombra, leve
sombra de una hoja, la serena
margen del mar, la momentánea espuma,
los antiguos caminos del bisonte
y de la flecha fiel, un horizonte
y otro, los tabacales y la bruma,
la cumbre, los tranquilos minerales,
el Orinoco, el intrincado juego
que urden la tierra, el agua, el aire, el fuego,
las leguas de sumisos animales,
apartarán tu mano de la mía,
pero también la noche, el alba, el día . . .

THE DAY BEFORE

Millions of grains of desert sand, rivers
that have never known repose, snowflakes
more delicate than a shadow, feathery
shade of a trembling leaf, the serene
shore of the ocean, the sudden spray,
the old paths of the bison on the plain
and of the true arrow on its way,
horizon after horizon, tobacco fields
and mist, the mountaintop, calm minerals,
the Orinoco, the elaborate game
weaving earth and water and air and fire,
mile after mile of docile animals,
all these separate your hand from mine,
but also nighttime, daybreak, sunrise, day . . .

—S.K.

UNA LLAVE EN EAST LANSING

A Judith Machado

Soy una pieza de limado acero.
Mi borde irregular no es arbitrario.
Duermo mi vago sueño en un armario
que no veo, sujeta a mi llavero.
Hay una cerradura que me espera,
una sola. La puerta es de forjado
hierro y firme cristal. Del otro lado
está la casa, oculta y verdadera.
Altos en la penumbra los desiertos
espejos ven las noches y los días
y las fotografías de los muertos
y el tenue ayer de las fotografías.
Alguna vez empujaré la dura
puerta y haré girar la cerradura.

A KEY IN EAST LANSING

for Judith Machado

I am a piece of cut and polished steel.
My irregular shape is not a random shape.
I sleep in a vague dream in a cabinet
I never see, bound as I am to my ring.
There is a lock that faithfully awaits me,
just one. The door is made of forged iron
and thick, strong glass. On the other side,
hidden yet no less real, is the dark house.
High in its shadows the deserted mirrors
look out on the empty nights and days
and at the framed photographs of the dead
and at the photographs' faint yesterdays.
One day I will be turned inside the lock
and push open the hard and heavy door.

—S.K.

ELEGÍA DE LA PATRIA

De hierro, no de oro, fue la aurora.
La forjaron un puerto y un desierto,
unos cuantos señores y el abierto
ámbito elemental de ayer y ahora.
Vino después la guerra con el godo.
Siempre el valor y siempre la victoria.
El Brasil y el tirano. Aquella historia
desenfrenada. El todo por el todo.
Cifras rojas de los aniversarios,
pompas del mármol, arduos monumentos,
pompas de la palabra, parlamentos,
centenarios y sesquicentenarios,
son la ceniza apenas, la soflama
de los vestigios de esa antigua llama.

ELEGY FOR MY COUNTRY

Its dawn was made of iron, not of gold.
It was forged by a desert and a port,
by a few gentlemen and the open
elemental landscape of then and now.
Wine and then war with the Spanish Goth.
Always bravery and always victory.
Brazil and the dictator. That headlong
history. Everything given for everything.
Red numbers for the anniversaries.
Pageants of marble, arduous monuments,
pageants of language, pompous parliaments,
centenaries and sesquicentenaries,
are scarcely ashes now, the charred remains
of what little is left of that old flame.

—S.K.

HILARIO ASCASUBI
(1807–1875)

Alguna vez hubo una dicha. El hombre
aceptaba el amor y la batalla
con igual regocijo. La canalla
sentimental no había usurpado el nombre
del pueblo. En esa aurora, hoy ultrajada,
vivió Ascasubi y se batió, cantando
entre los gauchos de la patria cuando
los llamó una divisa a la patriada.
Fue muchos hombres. Fue el cantor y el coro;
por el río del tiempo fue Proteo.
Fue soldado en la azul Montevideo
y en California, buscador de oro.
Fue suya la alegría de una espada
en la mañana. Hoy somos noche y nada.

1975

HILARIO ASCASUBI
(1807–1875)

Once there was a single happiness. Man
welcomed love as he accepted battle,
with the same pleasure. The sentimental
rabble had not usurped the good name
of the people. In that dawn, now insulted,
Ascasubi lived and fought, singing
among the country's gauchos back when they
were called an emblem of our nation's pride.
He was many men. He was singer and chorus;
he was Proteus on the river of time.
He was a soldier in blue Montevideo
and a gold prospector in California.
His was the joy of the flashing sword
in the morning. Now we are night and nothing.

—S.K.

MÉXICO

¡Cuántas cosas iguales! El jinete y el llano,
la tradición de espadas, la plata y la caoba,
el piadoso benjuí que sahúma la alcoba
y ese latín venido a menos, el castellano.
¡Cuántas cosas distintas! Una mitología
de sangre que entretejen los hondos dioses muertos,
los nopales que dan horror a los desiertos
y el amor de una sombra que es anterior al día.
¡Cuántas cosas eternas! El patio que se llena
de lenta y leve luna que nadie ve, la ajada
violeta entre las páginas de Nájera olvidada,
el golpe de la ola que regresa a la arena.
El hombre que en su lecho último se acomoda
para esperar la muerte. Quiere tenerla, toda.

MEXICO

How many things alike! The horseman and the plain,
The tradition of swords, mahogany, and silver,
The pious balsam that perfumes the alcove,
And Latin reduced to something less, Castilian.
How many different things! A mythology
Of blood that interweaves the deep dead gods,
The frightening prickly pear that haunts the desert
And the love of a shadow that precedes daylight.
How many eternal things! The courtyard filled
With slow and weightless moonlight no one sees, the withered
Violet pressed between the pages of forgotten Nájera,
The impact of the wave retreating on the sand.
The man who on his deathbed settles in
To await the end. He wants it, all of it.

— S.K.

EL PERÚ

De la suma de cosas del orbe ilimitado
vislumbramos apenas una que otra. El olvido
y el azar nos despojan. Para el niño que he sido,
el Perú fue la historia que Prescott ha salvado.
Fue también esa clara palangana de plata
que pendió del arzón de una silla y el mate
de plata con serpientes arqueadas y el embate
de las lanzas que tejen la batalla escarlata.
Fue después una playa que el crepúsculo empaña
y un sigilo de patio, de enrejado y de fuente,
y unas líneas de Eguren que pasan levemente
y una vasta reliquia de piedra en la montaña.
Vivo, soy una sombra que la Sombra amenaza;
moriré y no habré visto mi interminable casa.

PERU

Of all the things on the unbounded globe,
we scarcely get a glimpse of one or two.
Chance and oblivion strip us. For the boy
I was, Peru was the history Prescott saved.
It was also that shiny silver platter
hanging from a saddle and the silver
maté server with the snakes and the clash
of lances weaving a scene of scarlet battle.
Later it was a beach that twilight dims
and a patio's secret with trellises and a fountain,
and a few lines by Eguren on the wind
and immense stone ruins high in the mountains.
Alive, I am a shade shadowed by Gloom;
I will die not having seen my boundless home.

—S.K.

A MANUEL MUJICA LÁINEZ

Isaac Luria declara que la eterna Escritura
tiene tantos sentidos como lectores. Cada
versión es verdadera y ha sido prefijada
por Quien es el lector, el libro y la lectura.
Tu versión de la patria, con sus fastos y brillos,
entra en mi vaga sombra como si entrara el día
y la oda se burla de la Oda. (La mía
no es más que una nostalgia de ignorantes cuchillos
y de viejo coraje.) Ya se estremece el Canto,
ya, apenas contenidas por la prisión del verso,
surgen las muchedumbres del futuro y diverso
reino que será tuyo, su júbilo y su llanto.
Manuel Mujica Lainez alguna vez tuvimos
una patria—¿recuerdas?—y los dos la perdimos.

1974

TO MANUEL MUJICA LÁINEZ

The eternal Writing, Isaac Luria maintains,
Has many meanings, each authentic as the next,
True to Whomever is the reader, to the text,
And to the reading, and which each one preordains.
Your version of the fatherland, its splendid flourish,
Enters my darkness like the daylight entering
And the ode humiliates the Ode. (My rendering
Is only a nostalgia of ancient courage
And of ignorant daggers.) Now the Canto shudders,
Now the masses of a future and diverse
Kingdom whose gratitude and grieving will be yours
Surge forward, hardly burdened by the poem's fetters.
Manuel Mujica Láinez, once we both embraced
A fatherland—remember?—which we have misplaced.

—E.M.

EL INQUISIDOR

Pude haber sido un mártir. Fui un verdugo.
Purifiqué las almas con el fuego.
Para salvar la mía, busqué el ruego,
el cilicio, las lágrimas y el yugo.
En los autos de fe vi lo que había
sentenciado mi lengua. Las piadosas
hogueras y las carnes dolorosas,
el hedor, el clamor y la agonía.
He muerto. He olvidado a los que gimen,
pero sé que este vil remordimiento
es un crimen que sumo al otro crimen
y que a los dos ha de arrastrar el viento
del tiempo, que es más largo que el pecado
y que la contrición. Los he gastado.

THE INQUISITOR

I could have been a martyr. I was a scourge.
I purified other men's souls with fire.
Then, to save my own, I turned to prayer,
the hair shirt, wailing, tears and the yoke.
In the autos-da-fé I saw what my tongue
had put to death. I saw the righteous
pyres blazing and the tortured flesh,
the agony, the moaning and the stench.
I've died now. I've forgotten those who screamed,
but I know this vile feeling of remorse
is a crime I'm adding to my other crime
and that they'll both be swept clean by the wind
of time, which will endure longer than sin
and than contrition. I have wasted them.

—S.K.

EL CONQUISTADOR

Cabrera y Carbajal fueron mis nombres.
He apurado la copa hasta las heces.
He muerto y he vivido muchas veces.
Yo soy el Arquetipo. Ellos, los hombres.

De la Cruz y de España fui el errante
soldado. Por las nunca holladas tierras
de un continente infiel encendí guerras.
En el duro Brasil fui el bandeirante.

Ni Cristo ni mi Rey ni el oro rojo
fueron el acicate del arrojo
que puso miedo en la pagana gente.

De mis trabajos fue razón la hermosa
espada y la contienda procelosa.
No importa lo demás. Yo fui valiente.

THE CONQUEROR

Cabrera and Carbajal: these were my names.
I drank the cup of life down to the dregs.
I have lived and died so many times.
I am the archetype. The rest, mere men.

I was a wandering soldier of Spain
and of the Cross. I made war on untamed
lands of a continent that had no faith.
In hard Brazil I planted the first flag.

Neither Christ nor my King nor gleaming gold
were the driving force that spurred me on
to strike the fear of God in those pagan people.

The reason for what I did was the sword's beauty
and the tempestuous fight for its own sake.
Beyond that, nothing matters. I was brave.

—S.K.

EL INGENUO

Cada aurora (nos dicen) maquina maravillas
capaces de torcer la más terca fortuna;
hay pisadas humanas que han medido la luna
y el insomnio devasta los años y las millas.
En el azul acechan públicas pesadillas
que entenebran el día. No hay en el orbe una
cosa que no sea otra, o contraria, o ninguna.
A mí sólo me inquietan las sorpresas sencillas.
Me asombra que una llave pueda abrir una puerta,
me asombra que mi mano sea una cosa cierta,
me asombra que del griego la eleática saeta
instantánea no alcance la inalcanzable meta,
me asombra que la espada cruel pueda ser hermosa,
y que la rosa tenga el olor de la rosa.

THE SIMPLE MAN

Each dawn (they say) contrives new marvels, wonders
that can alter the most obstinate fate;
there are human footprints that have measured the moon
and insomnia can lay waste miles and years.
In the blue sky public nightmares wait to pounce
and darken daylight. In the world there is not one thing
that can't be something else, or its opposite, or nothing.
The simple surprises are what unsettle me.
I am astonished that a key opens a door,
I am astonished that my hand is a real thing,
I am astonished that from the Greek the sudden
Eleatic arrow can never reach its target,
I am astonished that the cruel sword can be beautiful,
and that a rose should have a rose's smell.

—S.K.

EL FIN

El hijo viejo, el hombre sin historia,
el huérfano que pudo ser el muerto,
agota en vano el caserón desierto.
(Fue de los dos y es hoy de la memoria.
Es de los dos.) Bajo la dura suerte
busca perdido el hombre doloroso
la voz que fue su voz. Lo milagroso
no sería más raro que la muerte.
Lo acosarán interminablemente
los recuerdos sagrados y triviales
que son nuestro destino, esas mortales
memorias vastas como un continente.
Dios o Tal Vez o Nadie, yo te pido
su inagotable imagen, no el olvido.

THE END

The old child, the man with no history,
the orphan who could as well have been a corpse,
wears out the empty manor house in vain.
(It belonged to both and now it is memory's.
It *does* belong to both.) Lost in his hard
fate, the suffering man seeks through his pain
the voice that was his voice. A miracle
now would be no more strange than death.
The sacred and the trivial memories
that are our destiny, those mortal
memories vast as a continent,
plague him endlessly and give no ease.
I ask of you, God or Perhaps or No One:
a lasting image, not oblivion.

— s.k.

A MI PADRE

Tú quisiste morir enteramente,
la carne y la gran alma. Tú quisiste
entrar en la otra sombra sin la triste
plegaria del medroso y del doliente.
Te hemos visto morir con el tranquilo
ánimo de tu padre ante las balas.
La guerra no te dio su ímpetu de alas,
la torpe parca fue cortando el hilo.
Te hemos visto morir sonriente y ciego.
Nada esperabas ver del otro lado,
pero tu sombra acaso ha divisado
los arquetipos últimos que el griego
soñó y que me explicabas. Nadie sabe
de qué mañana el mármol es la llave.

TO MY FATHER

You wished to die entirely and for good,
Your flesh and its great soul. You wished to go
Into that other shade with no sad flood
Of pleas from one whose pain and terror show.
We saw you die with that serenely calm
Spirit your father had before the lead
Of bullets. War gave you no wings, no psalm
Or shouts. The dreary Parc was cutting thread.
We saw you die smiling and also blind,
Expecting nothing on the other side.
But your shade saw or maybe barely spied
Those final archetypes you shared with me
That Plato the Greek dreamt. No one will find
That day for which your marble is the key.

                                — W.B.

EL REMORDIMIENTO

He cometido el peor de los pecados
que un hombre puede cometer. No he sido
feliz. Que los glaciares del olvido
me arrastren y me pierdan, despiadados.
Mis padres me engendraron para el juego
arriesgado y hermoso de la vida,
para la tierra, el agua, el aire, el fuego.
Los defraudé. No fui feliz. Cumplida
no fue su joven voluntad. Mi mente
se aplicó a las simétricas porfías
del arte, que entreteje naderías.
Me legaron valor. No fui valiente.
No me abandona. Siempre está a mi lado
la sombra de haber sido un desdichado.

REMORSE

I have committed the worst sin of all
That a man can commit. I have not been
Happy. Let the glaciers of oblivion
Drag me and mercilessly let me fall.
My parents bred and bore me for a higher
Faith in the human game of nights and days;
For earth, for air, for water, and for fire.
I let them down. I wasn't happy. My ways
Have not fulfilled their youthful hope. I gave
My mind to the symmetric stubbornness
Of art, and all its webs of pettiness.
They willed me bravery. I wasn't brave.
It never leaves my side, since I began:
This shadow of having been a brooding man.

                    — W.B.

BARUCH SPINOZA

Bruma de oro, el Occidente alumbra
la ventana. El asiduo manuscrito
aguarda, ya cargado de infinito.
Alguien construye a Dios en la penumbra.
Un hombre engendra a Dios. Es un judío
de tristes ojos y piel cetrina;
lo lleva el tiempo como lleva el río
una hoja en el agua que declina.
No importa. El hechicero insiste y labra
a Dios con geometría delicada;
desde su enfermedad, desde su nada,
sigue erigiendo a Dios con la palabra.
El más pródigo amor le fue otorgado,
el amor que no espera ser amado.

BARUCH SPINOZA

A haze of gold, the Occident lights up
The window. Now, the assiduous manuscript
Is waiting, weighed down with the infinite.
Someone is building God in a dark cup.
A man engenders God. He is a Jew
With saddened eyes and lemon-colored skin;
Time carries him the way a leaf, dropped in
A river, is borne off by waters to
Its end. No matter. The magician moved
Carves out his God with fine geometry;
From his disease, from nothing, he's begun
To construct God, using the word. No one
Is granted such prodigious love as he:
The love that has no hope of being loved.

— W.B.

PARA UNA VERSIÓN DEL *I KING*

El porvenir es tan irrevocable
como el rígido ayer. No hay una cosa
que no sea una letra silenciosa
de la eterna escritura indescrifrable
cuyo libro es el tiempo. Quien se aleja
de su casa ya ha vuelto. Nuestra vida
es la senda futura y recorrida.
Nada nos dice adiós. Nada nos deja.
No te rindas. La ergástula es oscura,
la firme trama es de incesante hierro,
pero en algún recodo de tu encierro
puede haber un descuido, una hendidura.
El camino es fatal como la flecha
pero en las grietas está Dios, que acecha.

FOR A VERSION OF *I CHING*

The imminent is as immutable
As rigid yesterday. There is no matter
That rates more than a single, silent letter
In the eternal and inscrutable
Writing whose book is time. He who believes
He's left his home already has come back.
Life is a future and well-traveled track.
Nothing dismisses us. Nothing leaves.
Do not give up. The prison is bereft
Of light, its fabric is incessant iron,
But in some corner of your mean environs
You might discover a mistake, a cleft.
The road is fatal as an arrow's flight
But God is watching in the narrowest light.

—E.M.

JUAN CRISÓSTOMO LAFINUR
(1797–1824)

El volumen de Locke, los anaqueles,
la luz del patio ajedrezado y terso,
y la mano trazando, lenta, el verso:
La pálida azucena a los laureles.
Cuando en la tarde evoco la azarosa
procesión de mis sombras, veo espadas
públicas y batallas desgarradas;
con usted, Lafinur, es otra cosa.
Lo veo discutiendo largamente
con mi padre sobre filosofía,
y conjurando esa falaz teoría
de unas eternas formas en la mente.
Lo veo corrigiendo este bosquejo,
del otro lado del incierto espejo.

JUAN CRISÓSTOMO LAFINUR
(1797–1824)

The volume of Locke, the shelves full of books,
the light of the patio with its checkered floor,
and the hand slowly writing out the line:
From the pale lilies to the laurel leaves.
When in the evening I invoke the chance
procession of my shadows, I see swords
brandished in public and ripping battles;
with you, Lafinur, it is something else.
I see you with my father arguing
hour after hour about philosophy,
and conjuring up that dubious theory
of some eternal forms inside the mind.
I see you correcting this very draft
from the far side of the mirror's doubtful glass.

—S.K.

NO ERES LOS OTROS

No te habrá de salvar lo que dejaron
escrito aquellos que tu miedo implora;
no eres los otros y te ves ahora
centro del laberinto que tramaron
tus pasos. No te salva la agonía
de Jesús o de Sócrates ni el fuerte
Siddhartha de oro que aceptó la muerte
en un jardín, al declinar el día.
Polvo también es la palabra escrita
por tu mano o el verbo pronunciado
por tu boca. No hay lástima en el Hado
y la noche de Dios es infinita.
Tu materia es el tiempo, el incesante
tiempo. Eres cada solitario instante.

YOU ARE NOT THE OTHERS

The writings left behind by those your dread
Implores won't have to save you. You are not
The others, and you see your feet have brought
You to the center of a maze their tread
Has plotted. Jesus' pain will afford no pardon,
Nor Socrates' suffering, nor the inviolate
Golden Siddhartha, who within the twilit
Final hour of evening, in a garden,
Accepted death. These too are dust: the soundless
Verb spoken by your lips, and the word written
By your hand. In Fate there is no pity
And the enduring night of God is boundless.
Your matter is time, its unchecked and unreckoned
Passing. You are each solitary second.

—E.M.

HISTORIA DE LA NOCHE

HISTORY OF THE NIGHT

(1977)

CAJA DE MÚSICA

Música del Japón. Avaramente
de la clepsidra se desprenden gotas
de lenta miel o de invisible oro
que en el tiempo repiten una trama
eterna y frágil, misteriosa y clara.
Temo que cada una sea la última.
Son un ayer que vuelve. ¿De qué templo,
de qué leve jardín en la montaña,
de qué vigilias ante un mar que ignoro,
de qué pudor de la melancolía,
de qué perdida y rescatada tarde
llegan a mí, su porvenir remoto?
No lo sabré. No importa. En esa música
yo soy. Yo quiero ser. Yo me desangro.

MUSIC BOX

Music of Japan. Drops of slow honey
Or of invisible gold are dispersed
In a miserly way from a water clock,
And repeat in time a weaving that is
Eternal, fragile, mysterious, and clear.
I fear that each one may be the last.
It's a past coming back. From what temple,
From what fresh garden in the mountain,
From what vigil before an unknown sea,
From what shyness of melancholy,
From what lost and ransomed afternoon
Does its remote future come to me?
I cannot know. No matter. I am
In that music. I want to be. I bleed.

—W.B.

BUENOS AIRES, 1899

El aljibe. En el fondo la tortuga.
Sobre el patio la vaga astronomía
del niño. La heredada platería
que se espeja en el ébano. La fuga
del tiempo, que al principio nunca pasa.
Un sable que ha servido en el desierto.
Un grave rostro militar y muerto.
El húmedo zaguán. La vieja casa.
En el patio que fue de los esclavos
la sombra de la parra se aboveda.
Silba un trasnochador por la vereda.
En la alcancía duermen los centavos.
Nada. Sólo esa pobre medianía
que buscan el olvido y la elegía.

BUENOS AIRES, 1899

The water well. The turtle at the bottom.
Above the patio the little boy's
hazy astronomy. The inherited
silver shop reflected in ebony.
The flight of time, which at first never goes by.
A saber that served in the desert long ago.
A serious military face, now dead.
The damp entranceway. The old house.
In the patio that was the slaves'
the shadow of the grapevine forms an arch.
On the sidewalk someone out all night is whistling.
Pennies are asleep in the piggy bank.
Nothing. Just that poor mediocrity
sought by oblivion and elegy.

— S.K.

EL ENAMORADO

Lunas, marfiles, instrumentos, rosas,
lámparas y la línea de Durero,
las nueve cifras y el cambiante cero,
debo fingir que existen esas cosas.
Debo fingir que en el pasado fueron
Persépolis y Roma y que una arena
sutil midió la suerte de la almena
que los siglos de hierro deshicieron.
Debo fingir las armas y la pira
de la epopeya y los pesados mares
que roen de la tierra los pilares.
Debo fingir que hay otros. Es mentira.
Sólo tú eres. Tú, mi desventura
y mi ventura, inagotable y pura.

THE MAN IN LOVE

Mirrors, ivory handles, instruments, roses,
table lamps and the clean line of Dürer,
the nine numbers and the changing zero,
I should pretend that all these things exist.
I should pretend Persepolis and Rome
existed in the past and that a fine
sand took the measure of the parapet
the iron centuries gradually wore away.
I should pretend that weapons and the pyre
of the epic and the churning, heavy seas
have gnawed down the foundations of the earth.
I should pretend there are others. It's a lie.
Only you are. You, my misfortune and
my happiness, inexhaustible and pure.

—S.K.

EL ESPEJO

Yo, de niño, temía que el espejo
me mostrara otra cara o una ciega
máscara impersonal que ocultaría
algo sin duda atroz. Temí asimismo
que el silencioso tiempo del espejo
se desviara del curso cotidiano
de las horas del hombre y hospedara
en su vago confín imaginario
seres y formas y colores nuevos.
(A nadie se lo dije; el niño es tímido.)
Yo temo ahora que el espejo encierre
el verdadero rostro de mi alma,
lastimada de sombras y de culpas,
el que Dios ve y acaso ven los hombres.

THE MIRROR

As a child I feared the mirror might reveal
Another face, or make me see a blind
Impersonal mask whose blankness must conceal
Something horrible, no doubt. I also feared
The silent time inside the looking glass
Might meander from the ordinary stream
Of mundane human hours, and harbor deep
Within its vague, imaginary space
New-found beings, colors, unknown shapes.
(I spoke of this to no one; children are shy.)
Now I fear the mirror may disclose
The true, unvarnished visage of my soul,
Bruised by shadows, black and blue with guilt—
The face God sees, that men perhaps see too.

—H.R.

LA CIFRA

THE LIMIT

(1981)

BEPPO

El gato blanco y célibe se mira
en la lúcida luna del espejo
y no puede saber que esa blancura
y esos ojos de oro que no ha visto
nunca en la casa son su propia imagen.
¿Quién le dirá que el otro que lo observa
es apenas un sueño del espejo?
Me digo que esos gatos armoniosos,
el de cristal y el de caliente sangre,
son simulacros que concede al tiempo
un arquetipo eterno. Así lo afirma,
sombra también, Plotino en las *Ennéadas.*
¿De qué Adán anterior al Paraíso,
de qué divinidad indescrifrable
somos los hombres un espejo roto?

BEPPO

The celibate white cat surveys himself
in the mirror's clear-eyed glass,
not suspecting that the whiteness facing him
and those gold eyes that he's not seen before
in ramblings through the house are his own likeness.
Who is to tell him the cat observing him
is only the mirror's way of dreaming?
I remind myself that these concordant cats—
the one of glass, the one with warm blood coursing—
are both mere simulacra granted time
by a timeless archetype. In the *Enneads*
Plotinus, himself a shade, has said as much.
Of what Adam predating paradise,
of what inscrutable divinity
are all of us a broken mirror-image?

—A.S.T.

BLAKE

¿Dónde estará la rosa que en tu mano
prodiga, sin saberlo, íntimos dones?
No en el color, porque la flor es ciega,
ni en la dulce fragancia inagotable,
ni en el peso de un pétalo. Esas cosas
son unos pocos y perdidos ecos.
La rosa verdadera está muy lejos.
Puede ser un pilar o una batalla
o un firmamento de ángeles o un mundo
infinito, secreto y necesario,
o el júbilo de un dios que no veremos
o un planeta de plata en otro cielo
o un terrible arquetipo que no tiene
la forma de la rosa.

BLAKE

I wonder where the rose is that your hand
unknowingly uses to lavish intimate gifts?
Not in its color, as the flower is blind,
nor in its sweet, inexhaustible fragrance,
nor in the weight of a petal. All those things
are no more than a few of its lost echoes.
The real rose is very far away.
It can be a pillar or a battle
or a firmament of angels or an infinite
hidden yet necessary world,
or the joy of a god we will never see
or a silver planet in another sky
or a terrible archetype that doesn't take
the form of a rose.

—S.K.

EL ÁPICE

No te habrá de salvar lo que dejaron
escrito aquellos que tu miedo implora;
no eres los otros y te ves ahora
centro del laberinto que tramaron
tus pasos. No te salva la agonía
de Jesús o de Sócrates ni el fuerte
Siddharta de oro que aceptó la muerte
en un jardín, al declinar el día.
Polvo también es la palabra escrita
por tu mano o el verbo pronunciado
por tu boca. No hay lástima en el Hado
y la noche de Dios es infinita.
Tu materia es el tiempo, el incesante
tiempo. Eres cada solitario instante.

THE SPECK

You will not be saved by what was left
written by the ones your fear implores;
you are not the others and now you find
yourself in the center of a labyrinth
your steps designed. The agony of Jesus
will not save you, nor of Socrates, nor
strong, golden Siddhartha who accepted death
in a garden as the sun was going down.
Every word you have written turns to dust,
as does every word your mouth has spoken.
In Hades there is no such thing as pity
and God's night is endless and infinite.
You are made of time, which never ceases.
You are every solitary instant.

— S.K.

LOS CONJURADOS

THE CONSPIRATORS

(1985)

CÉSAR

Aquí, lo que dejaron los puñales.
Aquí esa pobre cosa, un hombre muerto
que se llamaba César. Le han abierto
cráteres en la carne los metales.
Aquí la atroz, aquí la detenida
máquina usada ayer para la gloria,
para escribir y ejecutar la historia
y para el goce pleno de la vida.
Aquí también el otro, aquel prudente
emperador que declinó laureles,
que comandó batallas y bajeles
y que rigió el oriente y el poniente.
Aquí también el otro, el venidero
cuya gran sombra será el orbe entero.

CAESAR

Here is what the daggers left behind.
Here is that poor thing, a dead man
known as Caesar. The metal blades
have opened all these craters in his flesh.
Here is the hideous, here is the stopped
machine that was used yesterday for glory,
for writing and executing history
and for the full enjoyment of existence.
Here also is the other one, that prudent
emperor who rejected laurels, who
commanded battles and directed ships
and whose reign extended over east and west.
Here also is the other one, the one
to come, whose shadow will cover the whole world.

—S.K.

SON LOS RÍOS

Somos el tiempo. Somos la famosa
parábola de Heráclito el Oscuro.
Somos el agua, no el diamante duro,
la que se pierde, no la que reposa.
Somos el río y somos aquel griego
que se mira en el río. Su reflejo
cambia en el agua del cambiante espejo,
en el cristal que cambia como el fuego.
Somos el vano río prefijado,
rumbo a su mar. La sombra lo ha cercado.
Todo nos dijo adiós, todo se aleja.
La memoria no acuña su moneda.
Y sin embargo hay algo que se queda
y sin embargo hay algo que se queja.

WE ARE RIVERS

We are made of time. We are the famed
parable of Heraclitus the Obscure.
We are water, not the diamond that endures,
what gets lost, not what finds repose.
We are the river and we are that old Greek
who sees himself in the river. His reflection
changes in the water of a changing mirror,
in glass that changes just the same as fire.
We're the vain river on its fated course
toward the sea. Darkness closes in.
Everything says goodbye and flows away.
Memory will never mint its coin.
And nonetheless there's something that remains.
And nonetheless there's something that complains.

—S.K.

LA TARDE

Las tardes que serán y las que han sido
son una sola, inconcebiblemente.
Son un claro cristal, solo y doliente,
inaccesible al tiempo y a su olvido.
Son los espejos de esa tarde eterna
que en un cielo secreto se atesora.
En aquel cielo están el pez, la aurora,
la balanza, la espada y la cisterna.
Uno y cada arquetipo. Así Plotino
nos enseña en sus libros, que son nueve;
bien puede ser que nuestra vida breve
sea un reflejo fugaz de lo divino.
La tarde elemental ronda la casa.
La de ayer, la de hoy, la que no pasa.

EVENING

The evenings to come and those that have been
are all one, inconceivably.
They are a clear crystal, alone and suffering,
inaccessible to time and its forgetting.
They are the mirrors of that eternal evening
that is treasured in a secret heaven.
In that heaven are the fish, the dawn,
the scales, the sword, and the cistern.
Each one an archetype. So Plotinus
teaches us in his books, which are nine.
It may be that our brief life
is the fleeting reflection of the divine.
The elemental evening encircles the house.
Yesterday's, today's, the one that is always there.

—W.S.M.

LA SUMA

Ante la cal de una pared que nada
nos veda imaginar como infinita
un hombre se ha sentado y premedita
trazar con rigurosa pincelada
en la blanca pared el mundo entero:
puertas, balanzas, tártaros, jacintos,
ángeles, bibliotecas, laberintos,
anclas, Uxmal, el infinito, el cero.
Puebla de formas la pared. La suerte,
que de curiosos dones no es avara,
le permite dar fin a su porfía.
En el preciso instante de la muerte
descubre que esa vasta algarabía
de líneas es la imagen de su cara.

THE SUM

Facing the whiteness of a whitewashed wall
that nothing keeps us from imagining
as infinite, a man sits down and plans
to trace with precise strokes of a fine brush
on the blank surface the entire world:
doors and scales, Tartars and hyacinths,
angels and libraries and labyrinths,
anchors and Uxmal, the infinite and zero.
And so he fills the wall with forms. Fate,
which can be generous with strange gifts,
allows him to persist until he's done.
At the exact instant of his death
the man sees that the vast chaotic scrawl
of lines has drawn the image of his face.

—S.K.

NUBES

I

No habrá una sola cosa que no sea
una nube. Lo son las catedrales
de vasta piedra y bíblicos cristales
que el tiempo allanará. Lo es la *Odisea*,
que cambia como el mar. Algo hay distinto
cada vez que la abrimos. El reflejo
de tu cara ya es otro en el espejo
y el día es un dudoso laberinto.
Somos los que se van. La numerosa
nube que se deshace en el poniente
es nuestra imagen. Incesantemente
la rosa se convierte en otra rosa.
Eres nube, eres mar, eres olvido.
Eres también aquello que has perdido.

CLOUDS

I

There cannot be a single thing which is
not cloud. Cathedrals have it in that tree
of boulders and stained glass with Bible myths
that time will soon erase. The Odyssey
contains it, changing like the sea, distinct
each time we open it. Your mirrored face
already is another face that blinked
in day, our dubious labyrinth of space.
We are the ones who leave. The multiple
cloudbank dissolving in the dropping sun
draws images of us. Ceaselessly will
the rose become another rose. You are
the cloud, the sea, you are oblivion,
and you are whom you've lost, now very far.

II

Por el aire andan plácidas montañas
o cordilleras trágicas de sombra
que oscurecen el día. Se las nombra
nubes. Las formas suelen ser extrañas.
Shakespeare observó una. Parecía
un dragón. Esa nube de una tarde
en su palabra resplandece y arde
y la seguimos viendo todavía.
¿Qué son las nubes? ¿Una arquitectura
del azar? Quizá Dios las necesita
para la ejecución de Su infinita
obra y son hilos de la trama oscura.
Quizá la nube sea no menos vana
que el hombre que la mira en la mañana.

II

High in the air these placid mountains or
the cordilleras tragic in their shade
wander, darkening day. The name in store
for them is *clouds*. The shapes tend to be strange.
Shakespeare observed one, and to him it was
a dragon. A stray cloud of afternoon
glitters, burns in his word, and we transpose
it into vision we still follow. Soon
we ask: What are clouds? An architecture
of chance? Maybe God needs them as a warning
to carry out His plan of infinite
creation, and they're threads of plots obscure
and vague. Maybe a cloud is no less fixed
than someone looking at it in the morning.

—W.B.

ON HIS BLINDNESS

Al cabo de los años me rodea
una terca neblina luminosa
que reduce las cosas a una cosa
sin forma ni color. Casi a una idea.
La vasta noche elemental y el día
lleno de gente son esa neblina
de luz dudosa y fiel que no declina
y que acecha en el alba. Yo querría
ver una cara alguna vez. Ignoro
la inexplorada enciclopedia, el goce
de libros que mi mano reconoce,
las altas aves y las lunas de oro.
A los otros les queda el universo;
a mi penumbra, el hábito del verso.

ON HIS BLINDNESS

At the far end of my years I am surrounded
by a persistent, luminous, fine mist
which reduces all things to a single thing
with neither form nor color. An idea, almost.
The vast and elemental night and the day
full of people are both that cloudy glow
of dubious constant light that never dims
and lies in wait for me at dawn. I'd like
to see a face sometime. I don't know
the unexplored encyclopedia, the pleasure
of all these books I recognize by touch,
the golden moons or the birds in the sky.
The rest of the world is for others to see;
in my half-light, the habit of poetry.

— S.K.

ENRIQUE BANCHS

Un hombre gris. La equívoca fortuna
hizo que una mujer no lo quisiera;
esa historia es la historia de cualquiera
pero de cuantas hay bajo la luna
es la que duele más. Habrá pensado
en quitarse la vida. No sabía
que esa espada, esa hiel, esa agonía,
eran el talismán que le fue dado
para alcanzar la página que vive
más allá de la mano que la escribe
y del alto cristal de catedrales.
Cumplida su labor, fue oscuramente
un hombre que se pierde entre la gente;
nos ha dejado cosas inmortales.

ENRIQUE BANCHS

A gray man. An unfortunate turn of luck
made one woman not return his love;
that story is the story of anyone
and yet of so many under the moon
it is the most painful. He must have thought
of killing himself. How could he have known
that sword, that bitterness, that agony
would be the talisman given to him
in order to be able to reach the page
whose writing will outlive the hand that writes
and the stained glass high in the cathedrals.
His labors finished, he was just a man
obscurely forgotten among the people;
he has left us things that are immortal.

—S.K.

DE LA DIVERSA
ANDALUCÍA

Cuántas cosas. Lucano que amoneda
el verso y aquel otro la sentencia.
La mezquita y el arco. La cadencia
del agua del Islam en la alameda.
Los toros de la tarde. La bravía
música que también es delicada.
La buena tradición de no hacer nada.
Los cabalistas de la judería.
Rafael de la noche y de las largas
mesas de la amistad. Góngora de oro.
De las Indias el ávido tesoro.
Las naves, los aceros, las adargas.
Cuántas voces y cuánta bizarría
y una sola palabra. Andalucía.

OF THE LOVELY AND VARIED
ANDALUSIA

So many things. Lucan who coined the line
of verse and that other man the epigram.
The mosque's dome and the arch's curve. The rhythm
of Islam's water along the promenade.
The bulls of the afternoon. The wild music
that is also ever so delicate.
The fine tradition of doing nothing.
The Kabbalists of the Jewish quarters.
Rafael of the nights and of the long
tables of friendship. Golden Góngora.
The treasure taken greedily from the Indies.
The ships, the steel blades and the leather shields.
So many voices, so much gallantry
and just one word for it all. Andalucía.

— S.K.

TODOS LOS AYERES, UN SUEÑO

Naderías. El nombre de Muraña,
una mano templando una guitarra,
una voz, hoy pretérita que narra
para la tarde una perdida hazaña
de burdel o de atrio, una porfía,
dos hierros, hoy herrumbre, que chocaron
y alguien quedó tendido, me bastaron
para erigir una mitología.
Una mitología ensangrentada
que ahora es el ayer. La sabia historia
de las aulas no es menos ilusoria
que esa mitología de la nada.
El pasado es arcilla que el presente
labra a su antojo. Interminablemente.

ALL THOSE YESTERDAYS, A DREAM

Insignificant things. The name Muraña,
a hand, its fingers tuning a guitar,
a voice, now in the past, that tells all evening
the story of some long-forgotten exploit
in a brothel or a courtyard, some dispute,
a couple of blades, now rusted, that once clashed
and someone left laid out, these were enough
for me to erect a whole mythology.
A whole mythology dripping with blood
that now is yesterday. The learned history
of classrooms is no less illusory
than that mythology of nothingness.
The past is clay shaped by the present's whim.
Then shaped again, and reshaped without end.

—S.K.

PIEDRAS Y CHILE

Por aquí habré pasado tantas veces.
No puedo recordarlas. Más lejana
que el Ganges me parece la mañana
o la tarde en que fueron. Los reveses
de la suerte no cuentan. Ya son parte
de esa dócil arcilla, mi pasado,
que borra el tiempo o que maneja el arte
y que ningún augur ha descifrado.
Tal vez en la tiniebla hubo una espada,
acaso hubo una rosa. Entretejidas
sombras las guardan hoy en sus guaridas.
Sólo me queda la ceniza. Nada.
Absuelto de las máscaras que he sido,
seré en la muerte mi total olvido.

STONES AND CHILE

I must have passed through here so many times.
I can't remember them all. The mornings
or evenings that used to be now feel
farther away than the Ganges. Reversals of
fortune no longer matter. Now they are part
of all that malleable clay, my past,
which time erases or art manipulates
and which no augury has yet deciphered.
Perhaps back in the dimness was a sword,
perhaps there was a rose. Interwoven
shadows now watch over them in their dens.
All that remains is ashes. Nothing else.
Absolved of all the masks that I have been,
dead I will be my own oblivion.

—S.K.

UNCOLLECTED
SONNETS

PEDRO LUIS EN MARTIGNY

Verdioscuro el paisaje tiene algo de tarjeta
Postal. Y los pinares nos escancian su gesto
De sumisión serena. Parece una careta
El sol que despintó la lluvia. Pero esto

Es cosa cotidiana: Largos cielos norteños
En el valle sufrido derramando sus mares
Han empapado el alma humilde de los leños
Y la de las casitas absurdas. Los pinares

Rompe de pronto un hombre. El paisaje se achica
Se borran las montañas, se desmorona el cielo.
Como un gran campanario su corazón repica.

Es Pedro Luis de Gálvez, rufián y caballero
Que viene con la frente fulgente como mica
Y con las manos plenas de poemas de acero.

PEDRO LUIS IN MARTIGNY

Dark green, the landscape looks like a picture
Postcard. And stands of pine pour us a gesture
Of serene submissiveness. The sun blurred
By rain resembles a mask. But then this

Is an everyday thing. Long northern skies
Spilling oceans into valleys that abide
Have drenched the humble souls of woods and the
Droll little cottages. Suddenly a man

Breaks through the stands of pine. The landscape shrinks,
The mountains are wiped away, the sky collapses.
Like a great campanile his heart rings out.

Pedro Luis de Gálvez, outlaw, gentleman,
He comes with a brow that flashes like mica
And hands overflowing with poems of steel.

—E.G.

SONETO PARA UN TANGO EN LA NOCHECITA

¿Quién se lo dijo todo al tango querenciero
Cuya dulzura larga con amor me detuvo
Frente a unos balconcitos de destino modesto
De ese barrio con árboles que ni siquiera es tuyo?

Lo cierto es que en su pena vi un corralón austero
Que vislumbré hace meses en un vago suburbio
Y entre cuyos tapiales hubo todo el poniente.
Lo cierto es que al oírlo te quise más que nunca.

Arrimado a la música me quedé en la vereda
Frente a la sola luna, corazón de la calle
Y entre el viento larguero que pasó arreando noche.

El infinito tango me llevaba hacia todo.
A las estrellas nuevas. Al azar de ser hombre.
Y a ese claro recuerdo que buscan bien mis ojos.

SONNET FOR A TANGO IN THE TWILIGHT

Who was it that said it all in a homegrown tango
Whose drawn-out, lovely sweetness made me pause
Under some unassuming little balconies
In that leafy neighborhood that isn't even yours?

All I know is that in its sorrow I saw a simple yard
Within whose earthen walls the whole sunset fit,
A place I'd glimpsed a few months ago in some slum,
And that I loved you more than ever, hearing it.

Caught in that music, I stayed there on the sidewalk
Facing the lonesome moon, the heart of the street,
In the relentless wind that came down driving the night.

That infinite tango pulled me toward everything.
Toward the fresh stars. Toward the chance of being a man.
And toward that clear memory my eyes keep seeking.

—S.K.

VILLA URQUIZA

Un huraño tranvía rezonga rendimiento
En la borrosa linde que los campos vislumbra.
Y una corazonada de lluvia apesadumbra
Este domingo pobre de arrabal macilento.

Una que otra chicuela sonríe su contento
De posibles piropos en la acera y encumbra
Un prestigio fiestero la placita que alumbra
Con limpidez de luces el turbio dejamiento.

De golpe un organito profundiza la tarde
Publicando en arranque de sonido viviente
Lo que en las hondonadas del corazón nos arde:

Urgencia de ternura, esperanza vehemente,
Carne en pos de la carne con silencio cobarde:
Burdo secreto a voces que unifica la tarde.

VILLA URQUIZA

A sullen streetcar grumbles its fatigue
At the blurred line where fields begin to loom.
And a threat of rain weighs heavy and sad
On this poor Sunday in a wan, hungry slum.

An occasional young girl smiles her pleasure
At possible sidewalk flirtations and brings
A festive illusion to the square that brightens
With its sharp lights the pall of neglect and gloom.

A sudden organ grinder deepens the dusk,
Announcing in a burst of frantic sound
What burns so hot in the depths of all our hearts:

A need for sweetness and love, an urgent hope,
Flesh pursuing flesh in cowardly silence:
A base, well-known secret that makes dusk one.

—E.G.

LAS PALMAS

En la ruidosa punta de veinte singladuras
Supo alistar con arte sorprendente la noche
Ese alivio de mares, ese manso reproche
A las olas derechas y a las tormentas duras.

Después en mi conciencia dejaron grabaduras
Entre zangoloteos bruscos de carricoche
El mercado y la torre, serenísimo broche
Juntando calles quietas y celestes alturas.

Algunos caserones pintarrajeados de ocre,
Unas cuantas plazuelas, orondas como altares,
El palmar cuya cima la suave noche encierra,

Alcores que altivecen la población mediocre . . .
En ese sitio el alma, quebrantada de mares,
Recobró la caricia familiar de la tierra.

1923

THE PALMS

At the noisy end of twenty long days
The night knew how to enlist with surprising art
That marine relief, that mild reproach
To the crashing waves and the violent storms.

Later my consciousness remained engraved
Amid the sharp rattlings of the covered carts,
The market and the tower, with the serene link
Binding the quiet streets and the sky's blue heights.

Some big old houses tarted up in ochre,
Some little plazas puffed up like church altars,
The row of palms whose crowns the soft night holds,

Hills that make average people proud of themselves . . .
Here is where my soul, split by high seas,
Recovered the familiar touch of land.

—s.k.

PARA LA NOCHE DEL 24 DE DICIEMBRE DE 1940, EN INGLATERRA

Que la antigua tiniebla se agrande de campañas,
Que de la porcelana cóncava mane el ponche,
Que los bélicos "crackers" retumben hasta el alba,
Que el incendio de un leño haga ilustre la noche.

Que el tempestuoso fuego, que agredió las ciudades
Sea esta noche una límpida fiesta para los hombres,
Que debajo del muérdago esté el beso. Que esté
La esperanza de tus espléndidos corazones.

Inglaterra. Que el tiempo de Dios te restituya
La no sangrienta nieve, pura como el olvido,
La gran sombra de Dickens, la dicha que retumba.

Porque no hacen dos mil años que murió Cristo,
Porque los infortunios más largos son efímeros,
Porque los años pasan, pero el tiempo perdura.

FOR THE NIGHT OF DECEMBER 24, 1940, IN ENGLAND

May the great bells thicken the ancient fog,
May the porcelain punchbowl flow freely with eggnog,
May the firecrackers rumble and boom until dawn,
May the light of the wood fire illumine the night.

May the storm of fire that assaulted the cities
Tonight be a lighthearted party for men,
May kisses be found under the mistletoe.
And may there be hope in your splendid hearts.

England. May the season of God restore to you
The bloodless snow, pure as forgetting,
The great shade of Dickens, and happiness resounding.

Because it's not even two thousand years since Christ died,
Because even the longest misfortunes are ephemeral,
Because the years pass, but time goes on forever.

— S.K.

LAS GUERRAS

Oscuro ya el acero, la derrota
tiene la dignidad de la victoria;
la arena que ha medido su remota
sombra las dora de una misma gloria.
Las purifica de clamor y euforia
crasa y convierte en una cosa rota
el arco jactancioso. Gota a gota
el tiempo va cubriendo nuestra historia.
Ilión es porque fue. El antiguo fuego
que con impía mano encendió el griego
es ahora su honor y su muralla.
El hexámetro dura más que el fuerte
fragor de los metales de la muerte
y la elegía más que la batalla.

WARS

Now that the steel is dark with age, defeat
has the same dignity as victory;
the running sand that measured their distant
shadows turns them gold with the same glory.
It purifies them of noisy and coarse
euphoria and turns the boastful bow
into a broken thing. Drop by drop
time goes on burying our history.
Troy is because it was. The ancient fire
the Greek set with his desecrating hand
is now its honor and its granite wall.
The hexameter lasts longer than the loud
clash of death-dealing metal against metal
and the elegy outlasts the battle.

        —S.K.

1984

Quiero olvidar los muchos borradores
a cuya difusión me he resignado;
quiero olvidar mi módico pasado
y gozar de estos años, los mejores,
de aceptada ceguera y de no avaro
amor inmerecido. Las naciones
del planeta me honran. ¡Cuántos dones
me depara el azar! Todo esto es raro.
Quiero olvidar la ensangrentada historia,
la espada y sus batallas, no el poeta
que dulce las cantó, no la secreta
música tutelar de la memoria.
Quiero cantar la patria: los ocasos,
las mañanas, las voces y los pasos.

Buenos Aires, 15 de setiembre de 1984

1984

I want to forget my poems' many drafts
to whose diffusion I've resigned myself;
I want to forget my mild-mannered past
and to enjoy these years, which are my best,
of blindness I've accepted, and no greed
for love I haven't earned. The nations of
the planet honor me. How many gifts
I have received from chance! All this is strange.
I want to forget our blood-drenched history,
the sword and all its battles, but not the poet
who sang of them so sweetly, not the secret
guardian music that holds our memory.
I want to sing about my country: sunsets,
mornings, voices and the sound of footsteps.

—S.K.

1985

No en el clamor de una famosa fecha,
roja en el calendario, ni en la breve
furia o fervor de la azarosa plebe,
la pudorosa patria nos acecha.
La siento en el olor de los jazmines,
en ese vago rostro que se apaga
en un daguerrotipo, en esa vaga
sombra o luz de los últimos jardines.
Un sable que ha servido en el desierto,
una historia anotada por un muerto,
pueden ser un secreto monumento.
Algo que está en mi pecho y en tu pecho,
algo que fue soñado y no fue hecho,
algo que lleva y que no pierde el viento.

1985

Not in the clamor of a famous date,
red on the calendar, nor in the fleeting
fury or fervor of the troubled mob,
the shy country lies in wait for us.
I can feel it in the scent of jasmine,
and in a face that slowly fades away
in a daguerrotype, and in that blurry
light or darkness of the farthest gardens.
A saber that served its duty in the desert,
a story jotted down by a man now dead,
these too can be a secret monument.
Something in my breast and in your breast,
something that was dreamed but never done,
something the wind takes that is never gone.

—S.K.

Notes

These notes identify references in the sonnets that are likely to be unfamiliar to the English-language reader. They are not intended as a comprehensive guide to the allusions in the poems—such a guide would have to be encyclopedic, or at least as wide-ranging as Borges's reading and life experience—nor as a key to their interpretation, but as points of departure for further inquiry.

xvi **Introduction:** With regard to completeness, the *Textos Recobrados 1919–1929* contains one uncharacteristically nonsensical "Hybrid Sonnet" ("Soneto híbrido con envión plural," page 242), a collaborative work attributed to the unlikely foursome of Borges, Leopoldo Marechal, Ricardo Güiraldes, and César Vallejo. The nature of this collaboration and Borges's contribution to it remain undocumented—and its style is completely anomalous in relation to other Borges sonnets—therefore it is not included in this volume.

7 **Susana Soca:** Susana Soca (1906–1959) was a Uruguayan poet who died in a plane crash when returning from Paris to Rio de Janeiro. The "tiger, Fire" in the final line alludes to Blake and speaks to Borges's lifelong obsession with the tiger as a figure of beauty, power, and violence.

11 **To the Image of a Captain in Cromwell's Armies:** Oliver Cromwell, English Puritan leader and Lord Protector of the Realm from 1653 to 1658, led a brutal campaign against Catholic rebels in Ireland.

13 **To an Old Poet:** The poet invoked is Francisco de Quevedo (1580–1645), Spanish master of many genres, notably the sonnet, and one of Borges's earliest and most enduring models as a man of letters. "Y su epitafio la sangrienta luna" is a famous line from one of Quevedo's sonnets, on the death in prison of Don Pedro Girón, Duke of Osuna. The first line of this sonnet alludes to another "old" but more contemporary Spanish poet, Antonio Machado (1875–1939), author of *Campos de Castilla*.

15 **Blind Pew:** Pew is a character in *Treasure Island* by Robert Louis Stevenson, one of Borges's favorite authors, to whom this sonnet's

closing lines appear to be addressed; Stevenson died "on other golden beaches," on the island of Samoa in 1894.

17 **Allusion to a Shade of the Eighteen-nineties:** Juan Muraña, legendary knife-fighter of the Buenos Aires suburb Palermo where Borges spent part of his childhood, is one of the signal figures of the poet's imagination, an outlaw archetype of physical courage and amorality.

19 **Allusion to the Death of Colonel Francisco Borges (1833–1874):** Francisco Borges, the poet's paternal grandfather, who died on the battlefield, represents for Borges the more respectable, patriotic, military aspect of physical bravery or heroism.

21 **The Borges:** "The last two lines of this poem refer to King Sebastian of Portugal (1554–1578), who led an ill-fated crusade to the Holy Lands and was summarily defeated at Alcácer-Quibir in North Africa. Legend had it that he survived this battle and would one day return." (Alexander Coleman's note in his *Selected Poems*)

23 **To Luis de Camoëns:** Luis de Camoëns (1525?–1580), author of the Portuguese epic *Os Lusiadas* (and also incidentally a master of the sonnet), is considered Portugal's national poet. His biography, which includes forbidden romance, street-fighting, exile, imprisonment, and military adventure, encompasses many of Borges's mythic literary ideals.

33 **A Soldier of Urbina:** "Miguel de Cervantes served as an ordinary soldier with the Spanish Army in Italy under Captain Diego Urbina in the early 1570s." (Coleman)

47 **Alexander Selkirk:** "The experiences of the once-marooned sailor Alexander Selkirk (1676–1721) were sources for Daniel Defoe's *Robinson Crusoe*." (Coleman)

53 **To a Minor Poet of 1899:** 1899 is the year of Borges's birth; he identifies with the struggle of this imaginary poet to render in verse his own obsession with the twilight hour.

55 **Texas:** In 1961 Borges came to the United States for the first time, to lecture as a visiting professor at the University of Texas at Austin.

61 **Snorri Sturluson (1179–1241):** Snorri Sturluson was an Icelandic poet, politician, and historian, author of the *Prose Edda*, a compendium of Norse mythology and treatise on poetry (which Borges translated), who was killed at his home in a political assassination.

63 **To Charles XII:** Charles XII (1682–1718), king of Sweden, was a famously aggressive military leader whose brutal campaign against Russia, Saxony, Denmark, and Norway in the Great Northern War resulted in the end of the Swedish Empire.

77 **Rafael Cansinos-Asséns:** Rafael Cansinos-Asséns (1882–1964), born in Seville, presided over a literary circle in Madrid when Borges arrived in Spain with his family in 1919. Cansinos immediately

became one of the young Argentine's most important and enduring literary mentors and models. Leader of "the Ultra," or *ultraísmo*, a neo-Romantic modernist poetic rebellion against the Spanish literary establishment, he was multilingual, cosmopolitan, polymathic, and Jewish by choice (discovering the name Cansinos in his readings on the Inquisition, he embraced his identity as a Jew). Cansinos made a profound impression on Borges the apprentice man of letters and continued to be a touchstone of intellectual integrity throughout the younger writer's life.

83 **Wine Sonnet:** This poem can be read in part as a response to and commentary on Edward FitzGerald's English translation of the *Rubáiyát of Omar Khayyám*, which Borges admired as an example of translation as inspired re-creation.

93 **Ewigkeit:** The title means "eternity" in German.

103 **Junín:** The site of a famous 1824 battle in Peru led by Simón Bolívar against the Spanish, Junín is also a town in Argentina on the northern outskirts of Buenos Aires where Borges's grandfather served in the Argentine army. From its founding in 1827 it was an outpost set up to defend *criollo* colonists against incursions by hostile Indians.

109 **A Morning of 1649:** The date in the title refers to the execution of Charles I (1600–1649), Stuart king of England.

123 **New England, 1967:** In the fall of 1967 and spring of 1968 Borges gave a series of lectures on poetry at Harvard, later collected in the book *This Craft of Verse*.

127 **Ricardo Güiraldes:** Ricardo Güiraldes (1886–1927), Argentine poet and novelist, author of the classic gaucho novel *Don Segundo Sombra*, was a friend and generous mentor to the young Borges.

133 **To Israel:** This poem was written in 1967 during the Six-Day War. "Red Adam" refers to the Hebrew etymology of the word Adam, which means both man and red. (See also page 117.)

135 **Acevedo:** Acevedo, Borges's family name on his mother's side, stands for his grandfather Isidoro Acevedo, who served in the Argentine military and opposed the dictator Juan Manuel de Rosas.

137 **"Knight, Death, and the Devil":** The title refers to the engraving *Ritter, Tod und Teufel* by the German artist Albrecht Dürer, which hung in the Borges family home for most of the poet's life. Borges's title is in the original German, and this sonnet is the first of two poems he dedicated to the Dürer print. (See *Selected Poems*, edited by Alexander Coleman, page 291.)

141 **To John Keats (1795–1821):** See the Introduction for an account of Borges's awakening to the enchantment of poetry by way of Keats's "Ode to a Nightingale," read to him as a child by his father. Borges's use of the word "Panic" as an adjective in line 13

("la pánica memoria") refers to Pan, Greek god of nature believed to be present in all things. *The New Shorter Oxford English Dictionary* suggests another possible allusion, to one of Borges's favorite writers, Robert Louis Stevenson, who is quoted as using "panic" as an adjective in English: "A panic selfishness, like that produced by fear."

147 J. M.: The initials may be those of Judith Machado, to whom Borges's early poem "La Rosa," from his first book, *Fervor de Buenos Aires*, is dedicated. (See also pages 210 and 211.) The reference to a "lost Paradise" suggests the initials can also be taken to stand for John Milton, whose sonnet "On His Blindness" serves as a model for two Borges sonnets of the same title in English (pages 143 and 275).

149 Religio Medici, 1643: The title is also that of the best-known work by Sir Thomas Browne (1605–1682), English writer and physician; the Latin translates as "a doctor's religion."

169 Swords: "Gram is the sword of Siegfried; Durendal is the sword of Roland; Joyeuse is the sword of Charlemagne; Excalibur, the sword that Arthur pulled from the stone." (Borges's note)

173 Alonso Quijano Dreams: Alonso Quijano is the name of the country gentleman invented by Cervantes who reinvents himself as Don Quixote. Lepanto is a Greek seaport where Cervantes lost the use of his left arm in the battle between Spain and the Ottoman Empire in 1571.

177 Proteus: Proteus, the shape-shifter of Greek mythology, was referred to by Euripides as a former king of Egypt.

193 In Memory of Angélica: Angélica de la Torre was Borges's great-niece, drowned in an accident at the age of four. The history referred to in the final line is that of Argentina in 1974, the year the poem was written, a period of political chaos and violence following the death of President Juan Perón.

205 Colonel Suárez: Manuel Isidoro Suárez (1759–1843), Borges's great-grandfather on his mother's side, was an Argentine military hero, a victor at the Battle of Junín in Peru in 1824.

213 Elegy for My Country: This poem, written in the mid-1970s (published in *The Iron Coin*, 1976), is one of several Borges wrote in dismay over the political violence wracking Argentina in the years after the death of Perón, when Montonero guerrillas and the ruling generals waged what amounted to a civil war (known also as the Dirty War for the military's brutal tactics against the civilian population).

215 Hilario Ascasubi (1807–1875): Ascasubi, Argentine poet of gaucho culture, was also a soldier and adventurer who represents for Borges, in the chaos of 1975, on the hundredth anniversary of his death, a nobler national identity.

219 **Peru:** William Prescott (1796–1859), American historian, is the author of *History of the Conquest of Peru* (1847), which Borges read as a child. José María Eguren (1882–1942) is generally considered the greatest Peruvian poet before César Vallejo.

221 **To Manuel Mujica Láinez:** "Argentine novelist, short-story writer, biographer, and poet born in 1910, Manuel Mujica Láinez is most renowned in the English-speaking world for his historical novel *Bomarzo* (1962)." (Coleman)

239 **Juan Crisóstomo Lafinur (1797–1824):** Lafinur, one of Argentina's first poets, was also a pioneer in secular education and Borges's great-uncle. His arguments with Borges's father alluded to in the poem evidently took place in the young Jorge's imagination, given the date of Lafinur's death.

241 **You Are Not the Others:** See also "The Speck," page 259.

257 **Blake:** This poem is not technically a sonnet, but as the only 14-line poem in Borges's entire *Obra Poética* that is not formally a sonnet, it is included here as the exception that tests the rule, just as Blake, an otherwise formal poet, broke many rules of English prosody. Borges has many other poems of 13 or 15 lines, which appear to be deliberately not sonnets. Perhaps the closing lines of "Blake" provide a clue to the poet's intent here, with their reference to "a terrible archetype that does not take / the form of a rose," in much the same way as this sonnetlike poem does not take the form of a classical sonnet.

259 **The Speck:** See also "You Are Not the Others," page 241.

277 **Enrique Banchs:** Enrique Banchs (1888–1968) was a distinguished Argentine poet, master of the traditional Spanish sonnet, who published all his work between 1907 and 1911, after which he was silent as a writer, although he remained on the literary scene. Banchs was a figure of fascination for Borges, who may well have identified with Banchs's disappointment in love, and with such heartbreak as a "talisman" for the creation of immortal poetry.

279 **Of the Lovely and Varied Andalusia:** The title of this poem in Spanish adopts the Golden Age convention of referring to its subject as a woman. First-century Roman writers Seneca ("that other man [who coined] the epigram") and his nephew Lucan were born in Córdoba, intellectual capital of Andalucía. Córdoba was also the native city of Luis de Góngora (1561–1627), whose baroque extravagance of style became a model for Spain's famed Generation of 1927 (Alberti, Aleixandre, Cernuda, García Lorca, Guillén, Salinas, et al.) in their rebellion against the "pure poetry" of Juan Ramón Jiménez and Antonio Machado. "Rafael of the nights and of the long / tables of friendship" is Rafael Cansinos-Asséns of Seville, leader of the Ultra movement immediately preceding the

breakthroughs of the Generation of 1927, most of whose members were also Andalusians. See page 77 (and its note).

287 **Pedro Luis in Martigny:** Pedro Luis de Gálvez (1882–1940), Spanish poet and friend of the young Borges, lived the kind of reckless, adventurous life that the bookish and myopic Borges always envied and admired. This poem is, after his adolescent exercises in English and French, Borges's first known sonnet in Spanish. It was not published until 1987, but was written in 1920 and enclosed in a letter to his friend Maurice Abramowicz in Geneva. In the letter Borges describes it as a "classical sonnet . . . perpetrated by me—oh, unconfessable crime!—as a kind of exercise."

289 **Sonnet for a Tango in the Twilight:** Published in 1926 in the Buenos Aires journal *Caras y Caretas*, this poem was not included in any of Borges's books, though it is typical in some ways of earlier and later nostalgic evocations of nightfall in Buenos Aires. It is worth noting that the poet at this time was otherwise devoted almost exclusively to writing in free verse, which may explain the exclusion of the sonnet from collection in a book until the posthumous *Textos Recobrados 1919–1929*.

291 **Villa Urquiza:** This poem, published in the magazine *Alfar* in 1926, evokes the Buenos Aires neighborhood named in the title.

293 **The Palms:** The poem is dated 1923 but appeared in *Alfar* in 1926.

295 **For the Night of December 24, 1940, in England:** This Anglophilic poem was published in the magazine *Saber Vivir* in Buenos Aires in the autumn of the Nazi air attacks on London.

297 **Wars:** Published in the Buenos Aires daily *Clarín* on October 8, 1981, the poem appears to have been written at the height of the ongoing war between the Montonero guerrillas and Argentina's military junta, though it addresses the theme in classical, historical, and archetypal terms, perhaps as a way of avoiding the censors. According to Borges biographer Edwin Williamson, "The international edition of *Newsweek* of January 12, 1981, was banned in Argentina because it carried an interview with Borges that was deemed to be too critical of the political situation."

299 **1984:** This poem was published in the Uruguayan magazine *Separata Jaque* in September 1984.

301 **1985:** Published in 1986 in the catalog *Borges. Biblioteca Nacional*, Madrid, this is Borges's last known sonnet, and very likely one of his last poems.

Index

Titles in English

Titles in Spanish

Printed in the United States
by Baker & Taylor Publisher Services